04-16

DATE DUE

APR 27 2016			
			PRINTED IN U.S.A.

By Kathryn Harrison

True Crimes

True Crimes

A Family Album

. . .

Kathryn Harrison

R A N D O M   H O U S E / N E W   Y O R K

Published in the United States by Random House, an imprint and division of
Penguin Random House LLC, New York.

RANDOM HOUSE and the HOUSE colophon are registered trademarks of
Penguin Random House LLC.

The publication histories for the essays in this work begin on page 221.

Library of Congress Cataloging-in-Publication Data
Harrison, Kathryn.
True crimes: a family album / Kathryn Harrison.
pages cm
ISBN 978-1-4000-6348-2
eBook ISBN 978-0-8129-8850-5
1. Harrison, Kathryn—Family. 2. Authors, American—20th century—
Family relationships. I. Title.
PS3558.A67136Z46 2016
813'.54—dc23 2015009484
[B]

Printed in the United States of America on acid-free paper

randomhousebooks.com

2 4 6 8 9 7 5 3 1

First Edition

Book design by Susan Turner

For Katherine

Author's Note

Written over the course of ten years, these essays are sequenced to be read in order. To avoid redundancies, details of family circumstances have been excised after their first mention. Reading the essays out of order may inspire a little confusion, as later pieces lack information that appeared in earlier ones.

Contents

True Crimes

A Tale of Two Dogs

BITE ME. I OFFER MY HAND TO THE MONGREL CHAINED TO A pole outside the neighborhood locksmith's shop. It's a big dog, with pricked ears, a black face, and a mostly black coat. A shepherd mix, I think. Neglected, if not intentionally mistreated. Its tail is hairless on one side, and its long fur is matted and dirty. It should weigh a good seventy or eighty pounds, but it can't be more than sixty. A pariah of a dog, repellent in its ill-tempered misery. The kind of animal around which I'd make a wide berth, were I walking with my children.

The dog's growl is low, almost lost amid the clamor of the city: the approach of a garbage truck; the metallic shriek of an unoiled security gate; the rumble of a subway train I don't hear so much as feel through the soles of my shoes. I should be home at my desk, working. Instead, alone on the sidewalk, no passersby to witness, I hunker down until I'm eye-level with the animal and stretch my hand out farther, close enough to touch its nose.

Bite me. Do it. I deserve it. I don't say the words aloud, but I think them. Think them hard enough—if effort is what's required—to force them from human to canine brain, looking the dog in its dark, almond-shaped eyes. The left one is rheumy and dull, half closed over a crescent of wet fur. After a moment, it turns away from my outstretched hand and lays its head on its front paws, closes its eyes. This is the eleventh, maybe the twelfth cur that has refused to punish and absolve me.

Absolution. I am always seeking it, if not usually from dogs.

The dog problem began in Italy, the previous summer. Not that it seemed, in the beginning, to have anything to do with dogs. My mother-in-law found a Tuscan villa to rent—a farmhouse, but they call them villas—and my husband and I and our two children, six and four at the time, joined his parents for a month on the outskirts of Casole d'Elsa, a medieval village largely untouched by the intervening centuries. The photographs forwarded to us did little to convey the charm of the old house, two stories of yellow stone with a terra cotta roof, much of its façade hidden behind an immense trumpet vine in resplendent bloom, the bees hovering around it so gorged with nectar that they seemed to sink and stagger mid-buzz, too sated to sting or even threaten. The view from the grounds was of slanting vineyards and fields of sunflowers, crowds of black Cyclopean eyes fringed with golden lashes following the sun's transit across the sky. Fig trees laden with ripe fruit spread their branches over the pool, offering their sweetness to any swimmer who paused to reach for it. A patio was furnished for eating outdoors. The six of us made day trips to San Gimignano, Monteriggioni, and Siena, each place as lovely as the next. A perfect holiday, until I ruined it abruptly one night in the middle of dinner.

We were in Casole, at a tiny restaurant balanced on the periphery of the sloping plaza, gathered together around a white-clothed table set outside on the cobblestones, silverware polished bright and water glasses spangled with condensation, drops that caught the light like sequins. Not yet a week after the solstice, the June sun shone long past our children's usual bedtime, sending a spray of beams through the ancient pink crenellations that topped one of the towers in the village's fortified walls.

"I'm going back to the house," I said, apropos of nothing and interrupting the conversation.

"Why?" my husband asked, looking up from his menu.

"I don't feel well. I just want to go where I can lie down."

"What's wrong?" My husband and in-laws asked the question almost in unison. Did my head ache? Was it my stomach? Did I have a fever? Was I catching a cold? What could be wrong enough to send me home on so idyllic an evening, especially as all of us knew me to be stoic, often too stoic, with respect to physical discomfort? Thoroughly and successfully indoctrinated as a Christian Scientist from the ages of two until ten, I still had a hard time believing it wasn't my fault when I was sick: a manifestation of my having fallen into what Mary Baker Eddy, the church's founder, called "error," which separated humankind from God and left them vulnerable to illness and pain. Sick people were sinners. I never applied the conceit to other people. It was wrong and it didn't make sense. But with regard to myself, my first and often tenacious response to illness was denial. In fact, on that night in Casole, even I was surprised to hear myself admit what I'd refused to consider for weeks, well before we left for Europe: There was something wrong with me, and it was getting worse, not better.

"I'm fine, really. I just want to lie down."

"Do you want me to go back to the house with you?" my husband asked.

"No, no. You have dinner. I'll see you when you come home."

I set off through the golden dusk, thankful it was downhill all the way from village to farmhouse. Even so, I stopped several times by the side of the road, overcome by the beating of my heart, weirdly fast and erratic. Again and again it seemed to trip over its own rhythm; then it would shudder and restart. Each time this happened I ended up kneeling on the ground, having first bent over like an exhausted runner to put my hands on my knees, breathe, and will myself not to vomit. The only thing that got me to my feet again was the thought of my family walking back along the same road after dinner and coming upon me folded among the weeds in a ditch.

Once back in the house, its door left unlocked in this place of safety, I lay on the couch in the cool and shadowed living room. I used to be able to slow my pulse if I tried, breathing deeply and willing my heart to decelerate. The window across the room was a square of dimming light surrounded by the leaves of the trumpet vine, a green border shimmering in the gentle wind, and I tried to use it as a focus object, the way Lamaze classes had taught me to manage labor pains. But it didn't work, not at all. Inside me was the visceral equivalent of cacophony, as if every organ had slipped out of sympathy with the rest—the moment in a cartoon before a rattletrap engine blows and fails. I couldn't breathe, at least not as I was used to breathing; my heart was pounding so hard I felt it in my groin, my neck, my temples. I'd felt this way more than a few times over the previous month, but never so intensely or for so long. Until that night the feeling had been a fleeting thing, sensations endured and over with before I'd had a chance to analyze them. Once they'd stopped, I put them out of my mind. Told myself whatever it was, it hadn't been so bad, really. My problem was I needed to learn to relax. That's why I felt so tired and why I couldn't sleep. When we got back home, I told myself, I'd enroll in a yoga class. I'd learn to meditate. Something.

In the bathroom I lay on the cool stone floor. I was hot; maybe I did have a fever. I should have told my husband I'd fainted two days earlier, when, having decided I wasn't sick so much as stressed out and suffering from a lack of real exercise, I'd gone for a run. Not two miles in, I'd blacked out between two fields of sunflowers and discovered myself lying among stems as thick as my arms, looking up at their monstrous heads. I should have told him the gash on my heel, which bled so much it should probably have been sutured, wasn't from tripping on the stairs in the dark. I'd gotten up in the night to go to the bathroom, fainted, and cut myself on the sharp edge of a stone tread. I should have told the truth in Siena, that I hadn't, as I said, run back to the shop with the pretty paper but was throwing up over a drain in the alley we'd just passed through.

What I should have done was go to a doctor before we left for Italy.

"How'd it go?" my husband calls from work to ask me.

Back home the next month, all I do is see doctors. It's July in New York City: sweltering, humid. My husband has returned to work; the children have started day camp. I trudge from internist to endocrinologist to radiologist and back again.

"I'm radioactive," I tell my husband. "I come with warnings, protocols."

He laughs. "Protocols, huh?"

"You think this is funny?" I say. "No sex. No kissing. No sleeping in the same room with you or the kids. No using the same dishes. No touching the children. No sitting next to people on the subway. I'm not kidding," I say when he keeps laughing.

"For how long?"

"Most of the radiation is shed in the next forty-eight hours, but I'm not safe to be around for a week. Honey?" I hesitate. "Can we talk for a second?"

"We are talking."

"I just wanted to know if you had to get off the phone right away."

"Why? What is it?"

I'm pacing as we speak, first one way, then the other, tethered by the phone cord. "I did something you're not going to like," I tell my husband.

"Something aside from becoming radioactive?"

"Seriously."

"What?"

"I'm scared to tell you," I tell him. Then, after he sighs in exasperation: "I bought something. It was an expensive something."

"You bought what? How expensive?"

"I . . . it was after I left the doctor's."

"What is it?"

"I didn't mean to buy it."

"You bought something you didn't mean to buy and it was expensive?"

"Yes."

"Oh God. You bought a dog."

"How did you— Why do you think it's a dog?"

"You did, didn't you? You bought a dog."

"Why do you think it's a dog?"

"I'm right, aren't I?"

"Yes."

"What kind?"

"A puppy. She's so—"

"What kind of dog is it?"

"She's . . . she's . . . um . . ."

"She's what? What is she?"

"Well, she's a . . . she's a pug."

"You did not buy a pug!"

"I, um—"

"No! Do not tell me you bought a dog without talking with me about it! And especially don't tell me you bought a completely objectionable not-even-a-dog kind of a dog!"

"But you know I—"

"You know how I feel about little dogs!"

"Well, it's not as if anyone would expect you to walk"—*Or ever be seen with her,* I try to say, and the idea of my husband, all two hundred pounds of him, bearded, aggressively male, with a lapdog on a leash, is ridiculous, even—especially—to me. This dog has nothing to do with him. She's mine, not his.

"A dog is a golden retriever! A dog is a German shepherd! Or a collie! A boxer! An Irish setter, for Christ's sake! A dog is not the size of a rat!"

"Just because you had a golden—"

"I can not. I. Can. Not. Believe. We're. Having. This. Conversation."

"You're angry? I mean, I know you are, but are you very angry?"

"Hang on. I'm closing my door."

I hear the receiver strike my husband's desk with a smack, the sounds of his chair being pushed back hard, his footsteps, his office door not quite slamming, his body dropping— hurled—back in his chair.

"Yes! Yes, I'm angry! You knew I'd be angry! You can't just—you can't just buy dogs without . . . without our talking about it! Without talking to me! You. You—"

"I'm sorry. I'm sorry. I know you're angry. I didn't mean to buy it. It just . . . it just happened."

"It just happened? It didn't just happen."

"It did. I left the doctor's office, and I . . . I shouldn't have gone into the pet store, I knew it wasn't a good idea, but I couldn't help it. And I thought I was only holding her for a minute, you know, just to play with her because . . . I don't know, because I was feeling sort of . . . I don't know what I was. It was a little weird taking those pills, all the warnings. They came in a lead box. The doctor put on special gloves so he wouldn't be contaminated when he handed them to me, and then I had to swallow them. It was . . . I don't know, I might have been a little scared or something. Maybe I shouldn't have gone there alone. But it wasn't like I was looking for a pet store or even thinking about puppies. It was the furthest thing from my mind, buying a puppy, but then I passed this store and there were puppies in the window, playing, and I stopped to look and— Well, you know how they are, they put them in the window because they're irresistible, and I went in and—"

"I'm hanging up."

"Why? Because you're angry? I mean, is that how angry you are?"

"Yes. I am hanging up. I am at work. I cannot talk about this now. We'll deal with this later. When I'm home."

"Okay," I say. "Okay." I put the receiver gently back in its cradle. I can hear the children upstairs, laughing with the new puppy. We've called her Eloise, after the little girl who lives in the Plaza with her nanny, the little girl who never sees her rich, jet-setting mother and whose father is never mentioned once in any of the books by Kay Thompson. Eloise has a pug named Weenie.

The phone rings, and I hesitate before picking up the receiver.

"Take it back," my husband says.

"The puppy?"

"Take it back. I don't want to see it. I don't want it there when I get home."

"I can't. What about the children?"

"You should have thought about that before."

"They—the store, I mean—they won't let me. There's no returning—"

"We didn't even talk about how much the damn thing cost."

I say nothing. She cost a lot. A lot a lot.

"How much was it?"

"Too much?" I try.

"Christ! Don't tell me you can't return puppies to this store!"

"No, I don't think I . . . There was a contract I—"

"I'm hanging up. This is your problem."

———————

By the time the rest of the family came home from dinner in Casole, I was back on the couch in the dark. It was a clear night, and the window held a handful of stars. The children erupted through the front door, one chasing the other, and my husband shooed them toward the farmhouse stairs. Would his mother take them up and put them in the bath, he asked, so he could talk to me?

"Are you all right?" he said when they left the room, still young enough that they were easily distracted, young enough to believe their mother was invulnerable, immortal.

I shook my head no.

"No?"

"I want you to get a doctor," I said.

"But why? What's wrong?"

"I don't know. I don't know." He bent close to me. "I feel like I'm dying," I whispered to his face, surprised to hear the words but recognizing them as true. Seeing his expression, I started to cry.

"Does—does anything hurt? I don't understand."

"No, I don't know. It feels like something's . . . something's broken inside. I'm . . . my heart's beating way too fast and I can't breathe. And I threw up."

"Well maybe that's good, maybe it's food poisoning."

"It isn't, it's something else. I can't breathe."

"But you are breathing, sweetheart. You are. I'm watching you breathe."

"I know. I know. I just feel . . ." I reached out toward his chest, took his shirt, a piece of it, in my hand. "I'm . . . there's something really wrong. I'm sorry. I'm really sorry. I should have told you, but I didn't want to wreck everything—the trip. I thought I could wait until we got home. I'm sorry. Do you forgive me?"

"Yes, yes. Don't be silly. Now, just . . . just try to be calm, okay? Okay, sweetheart? Everything is fine. It's going to be. Stop crying, okay? Try to calm down. I'm going to talk to my mother. I'm going away," he said, freeing the front of his shirt from my fingers, "but I'll be right back, okay?"

I nodded. Proof, I thought to myself, that I wasn't exaggerating. I'd have to be dying to not be embarrassed by causing such a commotion. Suddenly everyone was running up and down the stairs. My husband went up and then down and then back up. His father would help get the children to bed. My husband came back down with his mother to call the local agent who had helped her find a house to rent. The agent called one doctor, then another, and another. Each time, after she got no answer, she called the house to report her failure. It was, after all, Sunday night.

"Get her to a hospital if she's that sick," the agent suggested. "I'll call for the ambulance."

Every day, I drive for hours on the Long Island Expressway. With me is a howling dog. A black Labrador retriever, six months old. I hate this dog, and I suspect he hates me. He should, because I will betray him. If not today or the next day, then soon. For now we just drive, east and then west. As we did yesterday, and the day before.

We drive all day, this black dog and I, drive and drive until it's time to retrieve the children from school. "How's Max?" they ask. "Can we walk Max? Can we take Max to the park?

Was Max a good dog today?" They pat and kiss him and I'm relieved that I've made it another day without disappearing their pet. Maybe I won't have to, I think, maybe things will change.

Exit 36. Port Washington, about an hour east from where we live in Park Slope, Brooklyn, an hour on the always-jammed expressway. I've driven the thirty miles between our house and the North Shore Animal League over and over and over again. Back and forth. There are days when I go twice, once in the morning and again at noon, making it back home just in time to pick the kids up at three. I put Max in the minivan, buckle my seatbelt, start the engine, and try to drown out the dog's howls, and my weeping, with the radio. The air conditioner isn't working, but the expressway is so choked with exhaust fumes that I leave the windows up and the car fills with a smell peculiar to nervous dogs, the one that's never quite masked by disinfectant at the vet's office. Within minutes the windshield fogs with the humidity of his howling and my crying. When I get to Port Washington, I park down the street from the shelter, rehearsing what I plan to tell them.

That the dog has been impossible to housebreak. We had him out on Long Island for six weeks and he was perfectly trained, peed outside, on the grass, but when we brought him back to the city in September he flipped. All he saw was sidewalk, no grass. And the fact that city sidewalks must reek of the piss of untold numbers of dogs does not, as I expected it would, assuage his apprehensions about the lack of grass. It does not announce to Max that this, this concrete, is the place for dog urine. I cannot walk a dog ten blocks to the park every time he needs to pee. So he pees on our carpets.

That he howls all night and the neighbors are becoming each day a little less forgiving. A few tenants in the apartment building behind our house scream obscenities at us in the dark; someone leaves anonymous, abusive notes in our mailbox, explaining how our dog has ruined his sleep, his work, his life. It may be he who has lodged "complaints concerning excessive noise from your barking dog" with the City of New York's Department of Environmental Protection. Max is, apparently, in violation of the Noise Control Code, which prohibits unreasonable noise caused by animals and allows for enforcement actions to be commenced against violators.

That, attractive and healthy as he appears, he is an overbred, highly strung, and neurotic animal. He jumps on my children, raking their arms with his toenails and tearing apart their clothes. He barks psychotically at my husband while my husband tries to read the paper. Just sits there at his feet and barks and barks and barks. "God damn this dog! What is wrong with him!" my husband yells. When he lowers the paper to look at Max, Max stops. As soon as he lifts the paper and tries to read, Max starts again.

"What. Does. This. Dog. Want!"

That the dog has disproved a conceit I've long cherished about animals and myself: that I can love any animal indiscriminately, without reservation. Animals are innocent by virtue of being animals. I've loved rats, snakes, horses, mice, fish, frogs, chickens, guinea pigs, tortoises, and, yes, dogs. I have raised a baby mockingbird, feeding it hourly with an eyedropper. I have played midwife to my grandmother's cats. I let them rear their kittens in my dresser drawers.

That this dog is the wrong dog, the completely wrong dog,

and not the one I wanted, not the one I picked out for myself, but the one I got in exchange for the one I wanted. My husband made me take the one I wanted back to the pet store, the pet store I should never have entered, given the state of mind I was in. I cried when I brought Eloise back. That's why they let me trade one puppy for another, even though I had signed a contract saying no returns or exchanges. When the saleswoman suggested my husband was a chauvinistic jerk with an impaired sense of masculinity—otherwise why would he object to lapdogs?—I didn't argue with her, I just cried.

That if I keep this dog I will have a nervous breakdown, a no-kidding, for-real kind of crack-up. This might happen anyway, but with the dog it's a sure thing.

These are all good reasons to get rid of a dog. But these are not good reasons for my children, who, despite their frustrations with his chewing and peeing, are children and love their big black, noisy, destructive, horrible puppy, no matter what he does. If I tell them I'm getting rid of him because he is too big a problem for me to handle, then they'll hate me. I will have done a thing they cannot forgive.

So, every day, I don't get out of the car with Max, I don't drag him through the door of the North Shore Animal League, the "world's largest no-kill animal rescue and adoption organization," according to their promotional materials. Instead I sit in the car with my forehead on the steering wheel and cry while Max howls long, shatteringly loud, Baskerville-caliber howls. He knows he's stuck with a person who bears him ill, a person on whom he is completely dependent and who is crying big fat Judas tears because she will forsake him. It's only a matter of time.

———

Later we laughed about the Italian ambulance, a white old-model panel truck equipped with only a bench on one side—no belts to prevent my husband and one of the two men who carried me out of the house from slipping nearly out of their seats as the van twisted through the hills—and a set of hooks and straps on the other, to which my stretcher was secured. It appeared to be, in essence, a knacker's wagon, a conveyance for collecting corpses in the aftermath of accidents. The burly man sliding with my husband from one end of the bench to the other chatted at us amiably without seeming to care that we didn't understand what he was saying. And if he didn't take my pulse or blood pressure or perform even the most rudimentary medical task, he did pat my arm every once in a while and call me *bella signora*.

My father-in-law remained at home with our children, and my mother-in-law followed the van from Casole d'Elsa to the nearest hospital, in Colle Val d'Elsa, winding up and down the narrow unlit streets, carrying a pocket dictionary to supplement her newly acquired Italian.

"Can you tell us what is wrong?" she asked the attending physician after I was transferred from the stretcher to a gurney in the emergency room. She spoke slowly and precisely—an actress, she has taught classes in voice—and held her pocket dictionary open to the page she'd just consulted.

He frowned, nodding. *"Il cuore . . .* How you say? *Il suo cuore batte . . ."* The doctor trailed off as my mother-in-law shuffled wildly through the pages of her little book.

"Cuore, cuore," she whispered to herself. "Her heart? *Cuore?* There's something wrong with her heart?" she asked the doctor.

"Sì, sì! Cuore, sì . . . Il suo cuore batte troppo veloce." He frowned meaningfully at her and leaned forward, speaking loudly. *"La signora è in condizione seria,"* he announced.

"It's . . . you're saying it's serious?" my mother-in-law asked.

In response, the doctor fished a scrap of paper from the pocket of his white coat and wrote on it before passing it over my chest to my mother-in-law, who stood on the other side of the gurney. My husband was stuck in the admitting office, dealing with the expectable insurance complications of my having had a health crisis in a foreign country.

"May I see?" I asked my mother-in-law after she looked at the paper, and she handed it to me. *"159 al minuto,"* it proclaimed in a controlled, feminine, and very tidy, un-physician-like script. 159? The last time my resting pulse had been measured by a doctor it was 56.

"Mon coeur?" I asked, pointing at the number, speaking French in the hope that it approached the Italian enough to make me understood.

"Parlez-vous français?" the doctor said with obvious relief.
"Oui."

The three of us cobbled together the doctor's few words of English, my very-much-in-disrepair French, and my mother-in-law's nascent Italian to arrive at the conclusion that my heart was beating dangerously fast—accelerating until it tripped over its own unsustainable velocity, and shuddered ineffectively before regaining a normal rhythm. *"Fibrillation atriale,"* the doctor pronounced it. I had a fever of nearly 40°C, or 104°F, and that I would be admitted to the cardiac unit.

"Pourquoi mon coeur battait si rapide?" Why was my heart beating so fast? The doctor shrugged, turned up his empty palms. He didn't know.

———

"You're not going to believe this dream," I tell my husband, trying to make myself heard over Max, barking at my husband, or at the newspaper in his hand. "It would be funny if it weren't so awful."

In the dream, I explain, the doctor who greets me at his office is not the same man as the one I met in reality two days earlier, the one who gave me two blue pills to swallow. "Where's Dr. Jameson?" I ask the dream doctor, who is younger, and much less creepy than the real doctor was.

"I'm Dr. Jameson," he says.

"Are you the son, then?" I ask.

"No. There's only one Dr. Jameson." He points to himself. "It's me."

"But . . . but when I was here on Wednesday, there was another doctor here. He said he was Dr. Jameson."

The young doctor frowns. "I don't have office hours on Wednesday," he says. "I'm at the hospital all day Wednesday."

"But . . . but a doctor was here. A doctor who said he was you."

The young doctor shakes his head, making a face. Clearly he doesn't like hearing what I'm saying. "Tell me, what did he look like, the man you say you saw on Wednesday?"

I describe the true-life doctor I met when I was not dreaming, the endocrinologist. He's tall and thin, with dry, papery skin. So dry that his fingers make a rustling noise when he rubs them together. He has wavy gray hair, unusually thick hair for an older man, and he combs it straight back with some kind of pomade. He was wearing a white lab coat, and glasses with thick black frames in front of his watery blue eyes. His eyebrows needed trimming. "He looked exactly like the doctor I saw," I tell my husband, "the real one, I mean."

"Oh God," the young doctor in the dream says. "Oh Jesus." He sits down heavily in the chair behind his desk.

"What's the matter?" I ask, suddenly frightened.

"He's—he's not a doctor. The man you saw . . . he's some . . . he's a crazy person. I had him locked up, but they must have let him out."

"What do you mean, a crazy person?"

"I mean crazy. Likes to pretend he's a doctor. He didn't do anything to you, did he? He didn't give you an injection or pills or anything?"

In the dream I start to cry. "He did," I say. "On Monday, he gave me an injection for a . . . a test he was doing. A scan. And on Wednesday he gave me two pills. They were radioactive, he said. That's why he had to wear gloves when he touched them."

"Radioactive! You didn't swallow them, did you?"

"He told me to!" I say.

"Are you insane? Are you out of your mind? You're as crazy as he is! He told you to swallow something radioactive, and you did!"

"Well, he . . . he was a doctor. He said it was going to make me—"

"He is not a doctor!"

"But how was I supposed to know that? When I came to this office, the other, the other man, the man who said he was you—he was here. How was I to know he wasn't you?"

"What kind of a doctor would tell you to swallow radioactive pills! This isn't science fiction, you know! This is medicine! How can you be so, so . . ." The doctor in the dream stops yelling at me. "I'm sorry," he says. "It's just that I'm scared, too. This guy almost ruined my career. I thought he was in a home for the criminally insane."

"But what about . . . what about the pills I took? What should I do?"

The young doctor shrugs. "Maybe they weren't radioactive," he says. "Maybe he was lying."

"They were," I say. "I know they were. They had that warning sign on the bottle they came in. The nuclear-hazard sign."

"Oh Jesus," the young doctor says. "Oh God. There's no way you're going to make it."

As it turned out, no one in Italy could figure out why my heart was beating so fast. I spent four days in the cardiac-care unit of the very old hospital in Colle, admitted long after midnight and installed in a bed vacated only minutes before by an elderly gentleman, the two of us wheeled flat on our backs past each other through the narrow corridor. The nurse, a nun in full floor-length habit, unplugged him from the heart monitor to which she then attached me. I was stricken as I saw that his beautiful white hair had been flattened by the pillow in some places, while in others it pointed every which way at ridiculous and rakish angles, like a punk musician's. Somehow it was his hair that demonstrated his vulnerability, suggesting I had usurped his rightful place in this old-fashioned, almost courtly hospital. But this sense of impoliteness was nothing compared to the guilt I felt the next morning, when his wife arrived, found me in the bed where she'd left her husband, and, assuming the worst, succumbed to hysterical weeping. She beat the foot of my bed with her handbag while I said, over and over, the only two Italian phrases I could remember while subjected to the torrent of her panicked raving: *Per piacere* and *Mi dispiace.* "Please" and "I'm sorry." Words that only exacerbated her distress. By the time one of the nuns arrived to explain, the distraught woman was so red-faced and breathless from the violence of her emotion I wondered if she might not be the next to be admitted to the cardiac-care unit.

I was not a good patient. Even before the beta-blocker and Valium restored my heart rate to something approaching normal—eighty or ninety beats a minute—thus reducing the other symptoms, I refused to use a bedpan and detached myself from the heart monitor to go by myself to the bathroom, setting off an alarm that summoned a scolding nun who literally threw her arms in the air when I didn't obey her command that I stay put in bed. Within the frame of her wimple, her fleshy face quivered with impatience and unchristian aggravation. Also in my disfavor was the fact that I was under her care without nightclothes or dishes or cutlery, none of which were supplied by the hospital. By the second night I had my pajamas, but at breakfast, lunch, and dinner the nun in charge of distributing meals sighed heavily when she had to find me a cup and plate and spoon, going out of her way, it seemed, to provide me with utensils that might shame me into acquiring my own: tiny spoons for babies, dishes painted with clowns and rabbits, cracked mugs that seeped hot tea onto my sheets.

Each day I was subjected to another series of tests and scans that revealed nothing, one requiring a trip by ambulance—another unequipped van in which I was strapped to a stretcher, as they wouldn't allow me to sit up for the ride—to a hospital in a neighboring town with a machine that could determine whether or not my aorta had a heretofore undetected aneurysm. But it didn't. My heart beat too fast, but it was without defect. I had an arrhythmia, an idiopathic tachycardia, a whacked-out, crazy American heart. The word *tachycardia* was one the doctor in charge of my case pronounced with a palpable relish, as if he found it an especially toothsome morsel of language.

"Your wife, she is a very nervous woman," he told my husband. "We see it all the time, these high-strung working women. They come to Italy to relax and, poof, they fall to bits." He said it again, *"Poof,"* releasing the affricative with an exaggerated, almost amused, and decidedly patronizing pursing of his lips.

"I want to get out of here," I said. "I want to be discharged."

"I don't think that's what happened," my husband said to the cardiologist, answering me with a placating stroke of my arm. My husband and the cardiologist spoke to each other from opposite sides of my bed, while below them I followed the conversation as I would a tennis match, back and forth, one side to the other.

"She is a nervous person, no?" the cardiologist demanded, and he answered himself: "Yes. The *signora* is very nervous."

"Not that nervous," my husband argued. "And she's in excellent shape. She runs—"

"Nervous, very nervous. Tightly—how do you say it? Tightly winded up?"

"Wound."

"Exactly. Very much so. Too tight."

"Being nervous can triple a person's heart rate?"

"Yes. Why not? Nerves can do anything. I am telling you, this is a syndrome with American women. They are—what is the way you Americans like to call it?—*stressed out*."

"Please just get him to discharge me," I asked my husband, pulling on his sleeve like a child. "Don't argue with him."

"She will be taking the pills I am giving her," the cardiologist said. "The beta-blocker, the sedative, and when she is arriving home everyone will be seeing she is fine."

I call my husband from home, breathless, crying.

"What happened? What's wrong?" he says.

"I lost the dog."

"What do you mean, you lost the dog?"

"I lost him. I lost the dog."

"Where?"

"In the park," I say. "I lost him in the park."

"Well, why aren't you there? Why aren't you looking for him?"

"I did. I have been for hours. It happened this morning. I was—well, you know how he won't pee on the sidewalk. I took him to the park, to walk him on the grass, so he'd pee. And then—you know how he is with loud noises—there were sirens, a couple of fire trucks went past, and he slipped his collar and bolted. And I was so fed up with him that I didn't really do anything. I mean, I didn't think he was running away, I just thought he was, you know, that he'd run a ways and come back. But he didn't, he didn't come back. He just got smaller and smaller. I was at one end of the long meadow, and he disappeared into the trees at the other end."

"Did you try calling him?"

"Of course I called him!"

"Oh Christ. Well, did you, I don't know, did you talk to a park-service person?"

"No. I didn't see one."

"Okay. Stop crying," my husband says, stern. "I'm hanging up. I'll call the parks people. You stay put until I call you back."

I replace the receiver. By evening we'll be making a flyer, taking it to be photocopied, taping it up all over the neighborhood. LOST. BLACK LABRADOR RETRIEVER. 6 MONTHS OLD. NO COLLAR. DOESN'T COME TO HIS NAME, "MAX." $$$ REWARD. The three of us calling. Walking. Crying, although not for the same reason.

The phone rings. "All right," my husband says. "I think you should go back to the park. The park service knows what happened, and they're looking for him, they've radioed the guys in their golf carts or whatever they use. They'll find him."

"What if he left the park?"

"They'll find him. Maybe you should go to where they have their headquarters—it's in the Lefferts mansion, isn't it?"

"Okay," I say. "I'll go." I hang up. I know they won't find him. They can't, because I didn't lose him in the park. Probably, though, I'm going to have to keep looking for at least a week.

The pills the endocrinologist prescribes for me are FedExed to his Manhattan office from a nuclear-medicine laboratory in New Jersey. They're on his desk when I arrive for my appointment, covered with bright orange stickers printed with the international warning sign for radioactive material, a black dot in the middle of three triangular shapes, like a stopped propeller. Before opening the box, the doctor puts on a pair of special blue gauntlets. Much thicker than latex exam gloves, they reach high up his arms and grab tight around the sleeves of his lab coat. From the box he extracts another, smaller box, inside of which is yet another box, this one of yellow plastic lined with an inch of lead. Inside this is the familiar amber pharmacy bottle, holding two gelatin capsules. Inside these is a dose of I-131—radioiodine—calibrated for me, based on the results of a scan taken of my thyroid two days earlier, after I was given a different, injected dose of the isotope, which allowed the endocrinologist to see the afflicted parts of my thyroid light up on a screen. It used to be that Graves' disease was treated by surgically removing the thyroid gland; current medical practice lets it poison itself to death, as it can't tell the difference between regular and radioactive versions of iodine, which it naturally absorbs from the bloodstream.

"Now," he says, folding his long, gloved fingers together. "You're going to feel worse before you feel better."

"Really?" I say. "I feel pretty bad already."

"Sometimes symptoms increase for a few weeks. As the thyroid cells die they release more thyroxine into your bloodstream. You'll have a sore throat and inflamed salivary glands for a few days. Maybe a week." He pauses. "Nausea, diarrhea, vomiting. The hand tremor could get worse for a bit," he says when I don't take the chance to speak. "Some patients report flu-like symptoms. Achiness, that kind of thing."

I nod, and the endocrinologist drops the two capsules into a paper cup and, still wearing his gloves, fills another with water. He sets the two cups before me. "Did you review the

protocols?" he asks, referring to the paper in my lap. I nod
again. I've read it twice.

- Arrange to have sole use of a bathroom for two days following treatment. On those occasions when you cannot use
  private toilet facilities, flush twice after each use.
- Maintain a distance of one meter (approximately three feet)
  from other individuals for up to three days following treatment.
- Arrange for any pregnant individuals or children less than
  two years old currently living at your residence to stay at a
  separate residence for three days following treatment.
- Avoid public transportation and limit personal automobile
  travel with others to only a few hours per day for the first
  two days following treatment. Keep as much distance as
  possible between you and other passengers.
- Avoid going shopping, to the movies, to restaurants, etc., for
  the first two days following treatment.
- Bathe daily and wash hands frequently.
- Drink a normal amount of fluids.
- Use disposable eating utensils or wash your utensils separately from others for the first week following treatment.
- Sleep alone and avoid prolonged intimate contact for one
  week. Brief periods of close contact, such as handshaking
  and hugging, are permitted. Sleep in a separate room for the
  first two nights following treatment.
- Launder your linens, towels, and clothes daily at home,
  separately, for one week. No special cleaning of the washing
  machine is required between loads.
- Do not prepare food for others that requires prolonged handling with bare hands for one week.

"Most of the radiation will be excreted in the first forty-eight hours after you take the medication," the endocrinologist says. "And most of it will leave your body in your urine. But traces will also be in your saliva and sweat and feces. Try not to touch your family members. Don't kiss your children. No intercourse with your husband for a week. No kissing him on the mouth, either."

"What about pets? What about my cat?"

"You can pet your cat."

"Can she sleep on my bed?"

He shrugs. "I wouldn't worry about the cat," he says, making it sound as if I have plenty to worry about already. "I want you to take it easy for the next month or two. No exercise, no housework, nothing that requires anything more than walking across a room."

"No housework? I have kids."

"Let someone else take care of them. Hire a sitter. Get a maid. I don't want you to push a vacuum cleaner, wash a floor or a window, cook a meal, pick up a laundry basket, nothing."

"For a month?"

"Two months."

"What's going to be happening to me that I can't do anything? What am I going to feel like?"

"Believe me, there's not going to be anything you feel like doing."

"I don't feel like doing anything now."

"Well, then you'll feel even less like doing anything. Multiply how tired you are now by ten. Just because you're no longer in a hospital doesn't mean you're no longer acutely ill. You are. The beta-blocker and the sedatives are masking how ill you are. You're lucky—"

"I know." I'm lucky I'm not dead. Especially as I was enough of an idiot to go running by myself in the heat in a foreign country when I was too sick to be walking from my bed to the bathroom. I tip the pills from the cup into my palm and swallow them with water from the other cup. It's done: I'm radioactive.

"I'll see you in a week," the doctor says, and I nod. In a week I won't be dangerous to him.

"Can I have that?" I ask, pointing at the lead-lined container that had held my pills.

"Why?" he asks.

"I don't know. I'd just like to keep it. A souvenir."

He smiles a sort of sure-wacky-lady smile and picks it up from his desk. "Let me wash it for you," he says, going to the sink.

"To get rid of stray radiation?" I ask. "How could that possibly hurt me?"

He looks at me meaningfully. "I was thinking of anyone else who might pick it up," he says, drying it with a wad of paper towels. "And of you, next week." He puts it in my hand, which, unready, drops under the weight of it.

"I know," he says. "I'm always surprised, too. Lead's heavy."

I leave the office on East 66th and turn left onto Lexington Avenue. I should turn right, toward the 59th Street subway stop, but I'm no good with directions even when not under duress. After a block or two, shifting the burden of the lead box from one hand to the other, I find myself stalled outside the window of Pets on Lex. Five puppies tumble and play among strips of white paper in the display pen. They're all little dogs—two Yorkies, a pair of dachshunds, and a pug about the size of a big baked potato. I watch them for a few minutes, reciting my pet store mantra, *Don't go in, Don't go in, Don't go in,* and then I go in.

There's a playpen set up for customers to interact with animals they're considering, and I ask one of the employees if I can please have the pug delivered to it. As soon as the puppy is in the pen I put down my lead box and pick her up, holding her close to my neck, feeling her delicious snuffling and wriggling against my throat, her wrinkled face pressed just over my poisoned thyroid. I can't be hurting her, I think—it will be at least an hour or two before I start leaking radiation. I hold her just in front of my face. "You," I whisper to her wrinkled black forehead, her bulging eyes, "have a face only a mother could love. And I do, I do love you." She slobbers on my eyelids, nose, and cheeks with her pink tongue, paddling the air with her little legs as if swimming toward me. I put her down in the pen and she somersaults over the carpeting inside, overfilled with happy, silly puppy energy. *You cannot have this puppy,* I tell myself. *You can't just go out and buy a dog on a whim. Besides, your husband doesn't like lapdogs. You know he doesn't.* I pick the puppy up again, tuck her head under my chin. I'd forgotten that wonderful feel of puppy skin, so soft and loose, buttery, with room to grow. *And you've always said you'd never buy a dog from a pet store. Puppy-mill dogs. Yes, she's cute, very cute, but she's probably overbred. And pugs have breathing problems. Just listen to her wheeze.*

I'm still telling myself why I can't have this puppy when the salesman returns. "Well?" he says.

I don't answer.

"Do you want to buy her? Because," he says, when I am still silent, unable to say the word I have to say—*no*—"if you don't want to buy this puppy, I need to return her to the cage with the others."

I stand, as if deaf and dumb, holding the puppy to my chest.

"It's store policy," he says. "We can't just have people come in to play with animals they have no intention of buying."

I never say the word. I just nod, holding the puppy as if she were already mine and no one could take her from my arms.

"Oh dear," my mother-in-law says over the phone. "The poor children. This will be the first great loss they experience."

I wince. "Do you . . . do you think it will be—I don't know—scarring?"

"Well, it won't be . . . I don't mean they're going to be damaged by it. But it is a big thing, losing a dog. What a terrible shame. And for you, too," she says, hearing me crying. "Are you feeling all right?"

"I'm all right, I guess. It's sort of hard to tell. Apparently it takes a while to get the thyroid level right, because of the way radioiodine works. Since it's been a couple of months, it's done most of what it's supposed to do—killed off most of the thyroid tissue—but it keeps destroying cells for a year, at a diminishing rate, so it takes at least that long for them to figure out how much of the hormone your body isn't making anymore, and how much of the synthetic thyroid hormone you have to take to make it up."

"But how do you feel? Do you feel like yourself?"

"I guess," I say. "Sort of." If feeling like a criminal is the way I usually feel.

"And the nervousness, the, um . . ."

"It's better," I say, answering her real question, about my emotional state, which, as the Graves' disease progressed, became ever more labile.

"It does impact your nervous system as well as your heart," said my internist, the first doctor to examine me when I got home from Italy. "The insomnia. The feeling agitated or restless, irritable. More than usually sensitive."

"How about more than usually nuts?" I asked him. "Crying over nothing? Not being able to concentrate? I just feel really weird. I think that's why—well, it's part of why—I didn't come see you in the spring. I didn't think there was necessarily anything physically wrong with me. I just thought I might be going crazy. And I wasn't . . . I mean, it didn't seem like you were the person to see about that."

He smiled. He was still holding the little rubber mallet with which he'd tested my reflexes, which were so "brisk" that I nearly kicked him in the face when he tapped my knee.

"Yes," he said, nodding to the specialist on the other end of the phone, ruffling the edge of his prescription pad with his thumb. We'd moved from the exam room to his office. "One fifty-nine. I'd say she's acutely ill. AFib. Hundred and four." He nodded. "Okay, then," he said to me, writing an address on the pad and tearing it off.

In twenty minutes, maybe less, I was heading downtown in a cab to an endocrinologist who had agreed to see me immediately. There wasn't time to waste, apparently.

I'm walking Max along Seventh Avenue, far south of my own neighborhood, when I come to a car service and go in the door. It's October, and the children are in school. What am I doing now, I think; what new craziness is this? I ask the dispatcher sitting behind the counter if he has any cars available. I'd just noted to myself that I was feeling almost optimistic, calm, this morning. Cleaned up the puddle of urine without cursing. Read the morning hate mail from the neighbors without succumbing to tears. In fact, as Max and I walked together down Seventh Avenue, I was just congratulating myself for having somehow passed the crisis point without an actual crisis.

The dispatcher puts down the greasy piece of aluminum foil he's holding, finishes chewing whatever's in his mouth. Bacon, it smells like. Whatever it is, Max wants it. He strains at his leash, whining, his toenails scrabbling for purchase on the dirty linoleum floor.

"Where you going?" the man asks.

"Coney Island," I say. *Huh,* I think. *Coney Island? Really?*

"Yeah, I got someone. He'll be here in a minute or two."

"Can I bring the dog?"

"He's not going to do nothing to the car, is he?"

"No. He's good. He's a good dog." Max emits an intensifying treble of frustration, running in place toward the smell hanging over the dispatcher's counter. I switch hands on the leash, holding it close to his collar.

The dispatcher shrugs. "If you say so," he says, clearly doubting Max's goodness.

It's just before ten in the morning, rush hour is over, and we fly along Ocean Parkway. "Nice day for the boardwalk," the driver says. "Nice day to take your dog for a nice walk at the beach." I say nothing. "And he's a water dog, too, right? A dog that likes the water. He's gonna have a great time, arncha, boy?"

Max answers for the two of us: a loud, thin wail that builds quickly to a *Tin Drum* whistle, loud enough to shatter the windows of this old sedan. I picture them blowing out, the sparkling spray of shards landing on the cars around us.

"Holy crap," the driver says. "He always do that?"

"Yes," I say. "That or something else. Something just as bad."

"Holy shit," the driver says, shaking his head, and he doesn't say anything else until we get to Stillwell Avenue.

"End of the line," he announces. He pulls up to the curb fast, coming to a squealing stop that sends Max onto the floor and me into the back of his seat. I hand the driver a twenty, wave away the change. "Thanks," he says, shouting over Max's howls. "Appreciate it. Nice day. Sunny," he hollers.

I pull the dog out of the car tail-end first, grabbing him around the middle. His nails leave long scratches on the vinyl upholstery. I give the door a good push closed and watch the guy drive off, accelerating away from us.

Max and I walk along the boardwalk and from there onto the beach. It's cold, despite the sun, and windy. There aren't many people around. As we draw closer to the water's edge, I expect Max—the water dog—to give some sign of enthusiasm, to be eager for a little romp in the surf. Instead, he leans back against the leash and plants his stiff legs in the sand, refusing to get his paws wet.

"Fine," I say. "Fine. Fine. Fine."

Back on the boardwalk, we head east, past the old freak show, boarded up for the season—the same freak show into which I once ducked with my children to escape a sudden cloudburst. My daughter was four, my son two, asleep in his stroller. We sat down to watch the man with no arms or legs roll himself a cigarette, light it, and smoke it, using only his tongue and lips. After that came the sword swallower and the lady in the bikini who danced around with a boa constrictor. She had so many muscles she had to be on steroids, a bodybuilder moonlighting on a different kind of stage. When the fire-eating lady, also in a bikini, passed a flaming torch over her legs and arms and midriff, my daughter leaned in to me and whispered, "Is she a witch?"

"Yes," I said, grateful to be provided this explanation I hadn't had to come up with. "That's why we can't do what she's doing," I added. "Because we're not witches." My daughter nodded, her eyes still on the fire-eating lady. "So you're not going to try anything like that at home," I went on. "First, because you're not allowed to turn on the stove or light matches, and second, because you're not a witch, so you can be hurt by fire."

My daughter looked at me, her blue eyes wide and grave. "I know," she said. "I won't."

"Can you promise me one more thing?" I asked her.

"Yes," she said.

"Can it be a secret that we saw this show? Can we not tell Daddy?" Can we not tell her father about my stunning lack of good sense? Because, after all, what mother in her right mind takes a four-year-old to a freak show?

"Daddy doesn't like witches?" she asked.

"No, not really. And I didn't know there was going to be a witch in the show. I don't want Daddy to worry about us seeing a witch. Even though she's not the kind of witch who can hurt us."

Max pulls against his collar so hard that he coughs. Anyone who bothered to look would know he hates me. The farther we go past Astroland, also closed for the season, the seedier the neighborhood becomes. Broken bottles glint among the weeds

in the abandoned lots. The boardwalk itself is derelict, missing
a plank here and there, inviting a fall. A clot of gangly teenage
boys huddles together on the periphery of one empty lot, as if
gathered around a campfire. Passing a joint, probably. They
look subdued rather than conniving. As we approach the
fenced-off end of the boardwalk, I unbuckle the collar from
around Max's neck. Suddenly, he's quiet. Stops whining and
steps closer to my leg. "Come on," I say. "Now you like me?
You don't. I'm not nice. Any one of these people here is nicer
than I am. You go find someone. How about that old guy sitting on the bench over there? He looks like he could use a
friend."

Max watches as I coil the red leash and collar around my
hand and stuff it into my pocket. "It's up to you," I tell him.
"You can run away if you want." I set off, doubling back, heading west now, and Max follows, heeling perfectly as he has
never done before. We walk back past the broken glass and
weeds, past the shivering juvenile delinquents, the old men
playing chess in their overcoats, the bundled, matronly wives
gossiping in languages other than English. Past a group of hardy
joggers, their bare legs reddened by the wind.

The dog and I walk on, westward, the sun behind us, cast-
ing our shadows before us onto the boardwalk. Perhaps my
husband does this, too. Perhaps he protects me from parts of
himself I would find disturbing. Doesn't marriage require this
unspoken promise from us all: to shield our mates from our
unexpurgated selves? Although I suspect most wives require
less expurgation than I.

"I wish you would just run away from me," I advise Max.
"I know things will work out for you. You're a handsome animal. You'd probably be happy here, near the beach. The guy

driving the car was right: You are a water dog. You should try it." Max trots on, panting a little, tongue hanging out. We turn up one of the side streets leading inland from the boardwalk, and he falls behind. In response, I pick up speed, my heart twittering with self-loathing. At this moment I am the worst person I know. Worse, in the future, every time I think of Max I'll feel just as I do now. Decades will pass; the feeling won't dull; it will cut to the quick.

I watch as Max looks around—doesn't he see me?—then crosses a parking lot, heading toward the open doors of the Shorefront nursing home. Its lobby is filled with people in wheelchairs or using walkers, a group of fifteen or twenty gathered as if for an outing of some kind.

Max trots directly into their midst, and I brace myself for a disaster of some sort. How is it that I, who once considered herself a kind person, am about to become a woman who, in the course of trying to lose her family's dog, kills off an as-yet-unknown number of grandparents? Imagining Max executing one of his usual leaps, raking skin, toppling walkers, shattering brittle bones, I find myself unable to move, every muscle paralyzed by horror, including those around my eyes, contracted into a wince.

But Max is, unaccountably, behaving. I am just close enough to see that he's thrusting his wet doggy nose into their wrinkled hands, their empty laps, wagging his hindquarters along with his tail. A few minutes go by and, oddly, no one evicts him. Instead of doing what I should, instead of going in and retrieving our dog, I sit on the low wall around the perimeter of the lot and wait. *Don't come back,* I think. *Please, please don't come back.*

Five minutes pass. The group assembled leaves for what ap-

pears to be a slow promenade along the boardwalk. I sit, waiting for something to happen, for another ten minutes. Finally,
I walk slowly across the parking lot, trying not to look furtive
and guilty, with the intention of peering into the lobby to see
that it is in fact as it looked from where I was sitting: empty,
save for a receptionist poured into a pink uniform dress, her
upper lip beaded with sweat. She blots it with a tissue and raises
her penciled-in eyebrows at me, standing on the threshold, between the open double doors.

I shake my head, taking her silent inquiry as an excuse to
stay silent myself. I return to the wall, mystified. Where did he
go? Is he on the boardwalk, or sniffing along some linoleum
corridor within the nursing home? What I should do is wait for
the return of the old people who set out on a walk, the group
into which Max had insinuated himself. Instead I get up and
walk hurriedly away, almost running, to the Q station, where
I board a subway train back to my neighborhood.

As soon as I get home, I call my husband at work. "I lost the
dog," I tell him.

"What do you mean, you lost the dog?"

"I lost him. I lost the dog."

"Where?"

"In the park," I say. "I lost him in the park."

Keeping Vigil

SEPTEMBER 18. WE'VE BARELY SETTLED INTO THE ROUTINE OF A new school year, our three children still chafing under our attempt to get them to bed whole hours earlier than we did during the summer. When the phone rings, at ten-thirty on this wet Thursday night, my husband answers with a sharp tone, quick to assume it's one of our older daughter's friends, calling too late on a weeknight. "Yes," he says after a silence. "All right." At the change in his voice I look up from the laundry I'm folding.

"Give him my love, okay? And tell Mom I'll talk to her in the morning." He replaces the handset in its cradle on the bureau. "Go back to bed," he says when he turns around. All three children are standing on the stairs outside our bedroom door.

"What is it?" they ask, almost in unison. "What's wrong?"

After a mostly sleepless night, the two of us get up early. I stand behind my husband, watching his reflection as he shaves around his beard. I can't find anything in his eyes beyond their attention to the razor. But when I hug him goodbye, his body feels different. It feels vigilant. As if his flesh has acquired consciousness.

During the afternoon, I find myself preoccupied by the picture I have of my husband in his seat on the train from New York to Washington, D.C. I see him among the Friday commuters, his work lying untouched in his lap. He stares out the window at the familiar scenery blurring past, the little houses with their fenced-in yards and laundry lines hung with clothes, the occasional bicycle lying on its side in the grass.

He calls from the hospital soon after he arrives in D.C. He's in the cafeteria with his mother and brother, he tells me. I hear other people's conversations, their laughter. His father will remain in the ICU for a few days. Morphine seems to be working a little better than OxyContin, and as soon as he's stabilized he'll be scheduled for exploratory surgery. Nothing in my husband's voice tells me how to feel. It's my mother-in-law's determined good cheer on the phone that fills me with apprehension.

For months, doctors have interpreted my father-in-law's relentlessly increasing abdominal pain, as well as changes in his bowel and bladder function, as the unfortunate result of radiation he received years before, in the aftermath of prostate cancer. Now, suddenly, his kidneys have failed.

A storm arrives after my husband and his mother get home from the hospital, and leaves much of Washington, D.C., without electricity. They use candles to find their way around the dark house. I picture them together, their faces lit by that inescapably devotional light. Can either of them have put a match to a candlewick without helplessly consecrating the little flame to my father-in-law, to his recovery, or to his release, to whatever is possible?

My husband calls the next morning. He's been up since five, he says. When his mother came to breakfast she found him in the backyard, raking up what the storm had blown down. Doing as his father would do, were he in good health and at home. Their shared awareness of this, of my husband's slipping into his father's role, must offer both of them comfort, and a measure of grief. In the past year, as his health continued to fail, my father-in-law asked my husband for some of his business cards to keep with him, in his wallet—like prayer cards, almost, talismans that demonstrate his son's currency in the world.

That my father-in-law's physical deterioration began with prostate cancer; that the surgery not only failed to remove it but also compromised his potency; that hormone therapy diminished the heft of his muscles and the hair on his body and face—for my husband, these assaults on his father's masculinity have felt personal, unnecessarily mean. They've hurt him, as gender-neutral ailments would not, and this aspect of his grief has shown me something of the primal, unarticulated psychic transactions between a father and a son—knowledge that arrived as an epiphany, making me feel foolish. Why hadn't I assumed my husband would have an experience parallel to

mine with my mother, to the indelible impress her breast cancer left on me? But then, I'm the only daughter of an only
daughter, raised in the absence of a father. Most of what I know
of men I've learned from my husband.

An explosive, stupid fight when my husband returns to New
York, a rerun of one of the stock two or three of our marriage,
but louder and more profane than usual. Whatever sets off the
conflict isn't the real catalyst—we know that. It's that even in
the absence of a diagnosis, this hospitalization is different from
my father-in-law's previous ones, the symptoms more omi-
nous. I go on crying long after we reach our exhausted truce.
My husband falls asleep, and I close myself in the bathroom. I
double over in the dark, press my face into a towel to smother
the noise I make.

The following day, as if by plan, my husband and I take the
afternoon off from each other, and from our anxious specula-
tions. He heads up to the park with our son, a football under
his arm. I go shopping with the girls, continuing our thirteen-
year-old daughter's quest for the perfect pair of jeans. I'm not
looking, but in Bloomingdale's I find a pair I like enough to
buy. "Hey," my daughter says when she sees them, and she
shows me the pair she's found: same style, same designer. Worried that this might spoil her pleasure in them—that proximity
to my mother-body might neutralize whatever hip qualities
they possess—I consider returning them to the rack. But she
encourages the purchase. I sign the receipt, aware that as much

as it's a record of sale, it also documents a wish: to be as my daughter is on this afternoon. To be as young, and as far from thoughts of death.

Here's what I don't know, not yet. The death of my father-in-law will leave me prey to concerns about my own father, from whom I've been estranged for most of my life. Having never attempted to contact him in the past twenty years, a few months after my father-in-law dies, I'll track down my own father's address. I'll pay an Internet company thirty-nine dollars and ninety-nine cents for the results of a "comprehensive background check," which will provide me not only the names of my father's relatives, associates, and neighbors, but also the banks, schools, and storage facilities in his community. Neither my mother nor I will be listed among his relatives, and I'll wonder how a person might go about erasing the records of such connections.

I won't call whoever lives in the house next door to his. I won't ask what he looks like, or if his hair is now gray. Does he seem to be in good health? Is he friendly, or does he keep to himself? What kind of a person do you think he might be? There's no limit, really, to the questions I won't ask. Instead, after many drafts, many misgivings, I'll send my father's wife a letter, wanting reassurance that no matter who he is, he does, in fact, exist. It won't be a long letter, just a request that someone please notify me in the event of his falling seriously ill. The subtext will be obvious—*give me a chance to say goodbye*—and the hostility of his reply to a letter addressed to his wife useful in that it will underscore the wisdom of our estrangement. We tried, and failed at, being father and daughter. That will not have changed. But for now my father-in-law is still alive—for a little longer; I am spared such preoccupations.

I don't know how much my father-in-law has given me in the years since I married his son. He'll be dead before I understand that all the fires he built, meals he praised, trees he planted, branches of buds he arranged on the table, and hugs he gave—especially those, tighter and longer than required for hello or goodbye—added up to something more than his affection for me.

Here's what I do know. I love him, unreservedly. Blood kinship could not make my feelings stronger. My father-in-law's thirty years as headmaster of a Quaker school has won him the respect of a great many people, as well as the love of generations of students who, as news of his illness travels, write to thank him for his presence in their lives. I'll read these letters, some of them out loud to my father-in-law, one recollection after another of his intuitively knowing and giving students what they needed, words and gestures that, somehow, made all the difference. One letter in particular will remain with me: a description of him walking home at the end of a workday and glancing up to see the letter's author sitting alone in the open window of his dormitory room. My father-in-law stopped walking to contemplate the boy. After a silence, he spoke. "You will be all right," he told him. These words, and their sincerity—spoken by someone else, they might well have sounded facile—changed everything for that student. Changed his life profoundly enough that, years later, he felt compelled to write and tell my father-in-law that somehow he'd heard the simple reassurance, and believed it. My father-in-law had been the catalyst for his transcending what had felt like hopeless confusion.

This quality of my father-in-law, his talent for silence, for feeling and understanding the state of another person's soul: Others must share it, but I don't know them.

So, yes, I love him. I love his generosity of spirit; I love that he isn't judgmental—not that he struggles and overcomes the failing, but that he doesn't judge. And I have a crush on him, one that began the day I met him, not long after my husband had learned my family history: an absent father, a teenage mother who left me in the care of her parents and who died when I was twenty-four. "Well," my husband said, and he took me in his arms, "I guess I'll just have to give you my parents. They'll be your mother and father, too." I heard it as a hope rather than a promise: generous, chivalrous, and not really possible.

But I was wrong. When we married, I wore my husband's mother's wedding dress, remade to fit me. At the end of the ceremony my father-in-law stood to read the Quaker marriage certificate, the first, after my husband and me, to announce that I was now a member of his family. Neither my mother-in-law nor my husband begrudges me the kind of crush I have on my father-in-law—benign, daughterly, reverent. Probably they know what I don't, that he is the only person who could begin to help me reassemble what my own father broke.

September 22, a Monday, 9:00 A.M. I return to the house after taking our younger daughter to school. My husband is sitting at the dining table, sitting very still, the cordless phone in his hand.

"Come here," he says, and I know from his voice, absolutely flat, that whatever it is, it's bad. "They operated late last night, because he was in too much pain to wait for them to schedule an exploratory surgery. It's cancer, and it's—it's everywhere."

We look at each other.

"Two," he says, answering my question, the one I can't ask. "Two months."

Silently, we stand from the table. It's as if we've decided to begin crying only in each other's arms. Sobs, very nearly inaudible, shake my husband's broad back. I've seen him cry, but rarely and never like this. The awful, intimate, and unfamiliar feel of his grief, his strong back heaving within the circle of my embrace—this is a thing I won't forget.

We go to the couch and sit together, repeating over and over what we cannot conceive, that my husband's father is dying, dying very quickly. Two months: a simple prediction. But we repeat the words as if they represent an impossibly complex formula we cannot understand. After a while we fall silent. Then, when we begin to talk again, it's of practical issues. We list every commitment we can postpone or cancel in order to free time to be with his parents.

"What can I do?" I ask my husband. I am his wife, and I love him—he knows that—but how can I possibly help him at a time like this? His answer is one I should know by now, one that always seems too simple to be true.

"Have sex with me every night. That will help. That will help with everything."

"It will?" I ask, having assumed that only something rare and difficult to provide could assuage grief as keen as this.

"Every night." He pulls me into his arms.

"Okay," I say, nodding my head against his chest. "Every night. I promise."

My husband's crying: What might relieve me of the physical feel of it—so much more wrenching to me than my own? I know my grieving; by comparison, his is exotic. It's like seeing a man embark on a walk across embers: How will he bear this, I find myself wondering; how will he stand the pain?

I keep losing track of the date, the month, even the season, and have to deliberately think my way back to where I am in time. And every observation, even the most pedestrian, is affected by my anticipation of bereavement. I can't clean out a closet or plant a flower bulb without thinking: The next time I do this, my father-in-law will have died.

Already I'm helplessly archiving memories of him, polishing and placing them carefully in my head, ready for retrieval. My favorites are of his intensely charming, look-at-handsome-funny-me capers, as when he did his silly, high-stepping, arm-swinging dance to make his grandchildren laugh. Or delivered a tragicomic monologue while holding up my husband's empty Christmas stocking, the year all the grown-ups focused so intently on the children that we overlooked one another. "Wait!" my husband said, and he got the video camera. As always, the little red light on the camera spurred my father-in-law to an even more delightedly ham performance.

As for fantasies of the future, all the Christmases and Thanksgivings and summer vacations we were to spend together; the graduations; the weddings; the trips—to Oaxaca, to the Galapagos; the party I was going to throw for my in-laws' fiftieth wedding anniversary: All these pictures and narratives have to be edited. As with writing a novel, the removal of a main character changes everything. All the stories I've told myself, told over and over, like bedtime stories, each one has to be reworked, reimagined. It's both automatic and exhausting; I get tired but can't turn it off.

I drop the lid to my grandmother's sugar bowl. It breaks into seven pieces, and I begin trying to glue them together. I should be packing my younger daughter's lunch, dressing her for the walk to school, but I can't wait to fix it, can't allow it to stay broken for even an hour. Over and over, the glued pieces come apart in my hands, and I grow increasingly tense, losing my temper at each setback, starting to cry with frustration.

"That has a doomed look to it," my husband says over my shoulder just as I'm considering throwing the lid away. But the word *doomed* makes defeat unacceptable. I waste more time regluing the pieces and wrapping the sticky, ugly mess in rubber bands. Four times it comes apart under the bands' tension; four times I start over. We leave for school a half hour late, the unevenly reassembled lid balanced on a paper towel on the kitchen counter.

I remember this involuntary shift toward magical thinking from the death of my mother, the mind taking every opportunity to fashion what amounts to a spell in order to reshape an unbearable outcome. How can I allow the lid to remain broken if there's a chance of repairing it? How can my husband permit even one of the trees his father has planted in our backyard to fail, when new branches and buds predict the spring, life emerging from what looks like death? If we align one small propitiation after another—and isn't this what's implicit in making love every night: our thwarting death with the act that conjures life?—if we make everything around us into a prayer, doesn't this represent some power, if nothing more than our refusal to accept what we don't know how to endure?

I wake early, at four in the morning. I try not to sleep away these quiet hours, before I have to rouse the children for school. My study is next door to our son's room, and before I go to my desk I look in at him, sleeping with his face wedged into the corner formed by the mattress and the wall. Although I straightened his room just the previous morning, the floor is strewn with baseball cards and bits of unassembled models, things I'll pick up later, before I vacuum. The house tends to be significantly tidier during a crisis; the solace inherent in setting things straight overcomes my usual disinterest in housework.

At my desk, I sit, staring out the window at the still-dark street. It's hard to work when I'm preoccupied by thoughts of my father-in-law in his chrome-railed bed, caught in a snare of tubes and wires, outside his room a corridor that never sleeps, never darkens. Perhaps he's awake, too, and it's just the two of us, alone and thinking.

Angiosarcoma, from the Greek, *angeion,* blood vessel, and *sarkoma,* fleshy excrescence. A rare and insidious malignancy that arises from vascular tissue, growing slowly, for as long as twenty years in the case of my father-in-law, and typically diagnosed too late to cut out or radiate or blast with chemicals. Twenty years. Twenty years would mean that when I met my father-in-law for the first time, his future, *this* future, was foretold. This future embraced me and I, unwittingly, embraced it.

Of course we knew it couldn't have been the return of his prostate cancer—my father-in-law's PSA levels were consistently low, too low for the cancer to have recurred and metastasized. Those exemplary PSA numbers encouraged physicians to dismiss his pain, weight loss, and the problems with his bowels and bladder—all of them classic signs of cancer—as "post-radiation syndrome," common among patients, like my father-in-law, who had received broad-spectrum pelvic radiation.

September 30, my first visit to my father-in-law. From now until his death, my husband and I will see little of each other, and we break our promise to make love every night. Typically, my husband will be with his parents from Friday night through Sunday afternoon and I'll spend two or three weeknights in Washington, relying on a babysitter to care for the children after school, while my husband is at work.

To make a 7:00 A.M. train to Washington I have to be on the subway by 6:00, where I sit with people on their way to work. Often, a number of them are in nurses' uniforms, as if all of us were traveling to the same destination, a vast hospice waiting at the end of a dark tunnel.

As a gift, I am bringing my father-in-law a delicate and unwieldy bonsai I spent a whole day acquiring: researching various species and their availability and traveling ninety minutes in either direction to get a perfect specimen, its little trunk beautifully gnarled, each tiny bough thick with dark, glossy foliage. On the train, I hold it in my lap.

When I arrive at Union Station, in D.C., sleep-deprived

and overwrought, I find myself walking toward the first of many absences to come. My husband's father isn't standing at the end of the platform, as he has for years, waiting for me with his arms open before I reach them.

At the hospital, the window in my father-in-law's private room has a view of woods, above them a bright sky. Next to his bed is a big convertible chair that can unfold flat to accommodate whoever stays the night with him, so he is never in the dark, alone. I drop my backpack on the floor—in it a book I won't read, work I won't do, pajamas I won't bother to change into. I set the little tree on the sill while I wait for a nurse to maneuver him into a position that is tolerable, a process so drawn out that it leaves enough time for my mother-in-law and me to hug and keep on hugging. When we pull away, it's without having spoken; neither of us has any words for this occasion. I dry my face, kiss my father-in-law hello, and rest my cheek against his. "There," I say, "that's good. I'm tired of loving you from afar." He smiles. It's a real smile, radiant and flirtatious.

"You're good at it, though. I can feel what you send me." How can I not answer his smile with my own when I see how happy he is that I've come? My mother-in-law leaves in search of coffee, and I take her place in the chair by the bed. When I look into his eyes I see that they're dilated from morphine, but it isn't enough. Enough would render him unconscious, unable to communicate. So he asks for less, and there are groans he can't suppress; he pants to brace himself against the pain. Already it has changed his face. How alike we all look in suffering: We bare our teeth in the same grimace, whimper the same whimpers, helplessly pick at the bedclothes.

————

Nightfall on the day I leave the hospital. In the taxi's rearview mirror I see the driver wincing in response to my uninterrupted crying; finally, he turns on the radio. At Union Station I catch sight of myself in a shop window and see that I look as I feel, exhausted and strung-out, like a child who's lost the hand she was holding.

It's nearly midnight when I get home. I leave my shoes by the door so I can run up the stairs quietly. I climb in bed on top of my husband, awake in the dark. Still in my street clothes, I shove my face into his neck, his beard prickling my eyelids. It's an hour before I let go of him long enough to undress.

I hang a string of lights over the double doors that separate our living and dining areas. They're unusual, each bulb painted so that it looks like an illuminated glass paperweight, the kind made in Italy and crowded with tiny flowers of many colors. I bought them the previous spring to celebrate a visit from my husband's parents, and hung them around the mirror over the guest room's mantel. My father-in-law, who loves candles and lanterns and holiday lights, was already frail enough to elicit our tenderness, a desire to provide every possible pleasure. The visit was timed to the Little League calendar; our son, nearly eleven, was to pitch in two baseball games that weekend, and my husband wanted his father to see him play. As it happened, the games were rained out, but it didn't really matter; they brought my father-in-law to our home for what would be the last time.

The lights are pretty in the new location, a festive counterbalance to the shortening autumn days, and because I bought them for my father-in-law, they have a private, votive quality.

I can plug them in, and no one need know that this, too, is a little prayer.

A Sunday night, October 5. My husband has just returned from another weekend in Washington. We haven't been able to agree on the right moment to tell the children about this illness that has required so many visits to their grandparents. I want to do it as soon as possible—I wish we had told them from the beginning—because I'm not good at disguising emotion, and already they suspect I'm hiding something. My husband wants to wait until they've had a chance to see his father, one that isn't made awkward by defining it as a goodbye.

And, though he doesn't say this, he wants to preserve a part of us, our family, that doesn't know what we know.

The children, however, settle the question for us by acting so obnoxiously at the dinner table that it seems as if they are trying to dismantle whatever poise we've maintained in the past weeks. Finally, after asking ten or more times for a little peace in which to eat, my husband strikes his open hand against the table and says he's had a terrible weekend and that all of them must shut up immediately.

"What was so bad about it?" our son asks.

"Granddaddy is very sick."

"Well, yeah, but he's getting better, right?"

"No. No, he is not. He is not."

"But, but he's not going to die or anything."

"He is. He is dying."

Abruptly, the clamor and fidgeting collapses into stunned silence. Our son puts down his fork and covers his face. Tears drip down from under his hands, which I notice have not been washed, fingers still grimy from playing basketball. Our older daughter turns to me, a complicated look of betrayal on her face, not one directed at me for having kept the news from her, so much as at life, at fate, at whatever *It* is that takes away what *It* has given us. This adult anguish is the property of her eyes. From the nose down she's the little girl she was at five or six; her chin wobbles as she tries to hide the fact that she's crying, a thing she tries not to do in company and is never willing to admit. Her little sister—ten years younger, she grants our older daughter the status of a parent, albeit an unusually fun one— gets up and goes to our son, her big brother, talking softly to him from outside the hands still pressed over his face. "Don't worry," she says. "It will be all right," and she repeats this over and over, she strokes his head and kisses his dirty fingers.

The incision gets infected. The surgeon who performed the operation, his scalpel cutting from just under my father-in-law's sternum, detouring around his navel, and continuing on down to his pubis to make an opening some twelve inches long, removes the staples holding the two sides together, and, after cleaning the wound, leaves it open to heal. On my next visit, when I arrive, I find a nurse bent over the bed, changing the dressing. I pause at the open door and knock.

"Come in," my father-in-law says. "I want you to see this." At this, the nurse looks up. She raises a gloved hand in protest.

"I don't know if that's—I don't think—"

"It's all right. She's interested in medicine," my father-in-law tells her. And I am. But the nurse was right. I only just manage not to step back in shock. My eyes fill with tears; I can't stop myself from covering my mouth with my hands. It's not—it can't be—that my father-in-law wants me to see what I'd find interesting. No, he needs witness to this, this hole, so long and deep that I think the word *seppuku,* Japanese for ritual disembowelment. A word that will never again seem literary and mannered, the property of an effete foreign novel.

"Oh," I say. "Oh God." I come to the head of the bed, take his hand and kiss it, hold it to my face. "A purple heart," I say. "Two." And then I say, "Never mind. A hundred aren't enough." Not enough to acknowledge what has to be the horror of looking down into his own split-open body, a gash that's red and glistening wet and so, so big.

Back home, I ask my husband not to look. "Not unless he asks you." And I tell him the truth: that it is worse than any wound I've ever seen, even in photographs. That my husband's looking at it can only hurt him, and to what end?

"Listen," I say to him the next night, before he leaves again for Washington. "Every day since I saw it," I tell him, "some of that day—some of me—disappears into that hole."

October 10. My father-in-law turns seventy-one. A tissue sample from one of his tumors is sent to the Mayo Clinic for analysis. I tell someone this and hear that "Mayo" tone in my voice, betraying both respect and desperation. It's as if I'm referring to Lourdes—a mythic destination of last resort, the best that secular gods can offer, the hope for a new, different interpretation: a miracle.

My husband has put two big tomatoes from his father's garden on the windowsill over the kitchen sink. They are ready to eat, almost overripe, but neither of us has cut into one. "Save the seeds," my husband says now. "Save the seeds from my father's tomatoes."

"Do I dry them out on a paper towel?" I ask, but he doesn't answer my question.

"You'll have to be prepared for some major relic collecting," he says, looking out the window. "Seeds, sweaters, shirts, pens . . ." He trails off.

But I don't need to prepare. I didn't part with my mother's old nightgowns until eighteen years after she died.

It's that many years and more since I've waited by the deathbed of someone I love. Still, how familiar it feels—as if a version of me, the girl keeping vigil, continues to exist, ever at attention, summoned when needed by the dying: my grandfather, my mother, my grandmother. I take my place in the chair by his bed, slip off my shoes, and tuck my feet into the warm seam between mattress and pad, careful to do it so gently that the bed doesn't even quiver. "Egg-crate," that pad was called when my mother was dying, the shape of the foam that helped protect a patient's skin from bedsores. My father-in-law's is state-of-the-art, filled with moving air, humming industriously, with a set of buttons to control its temperature and the degree of its firmness.

I fall into place beside my mother-in-law, each of us massaging a foot, providing whatever sensation we can to distract my father-in-law from pain, talking and talking about nothing, a quiet back-and-forth that he hears without listening, his eyes closed. "Don't stop," he says whenever we pause. "I like to hear your voices."

We allow ourselves to weep in the hall and then, immediately, without having to try, we stop as we walk through the door to my father-in-law's room. We resume our quiet conversation, our foot-rubbing, ice-chip-proffering, forehead-stroking, blanket-fetching, hand-holding presence. Our waiting. Sometimes, in the company of this man whom so many people love, their gifts and flowers and letters multiplying over every surface of his room, I find myself wondering what happens to people who don't have hands to hold as they die. Do they do it more quickly, so as to get it over with? Or do they linger? Do they wait to be touched?

"Worlds within worlds," my father-in-law says. He's trying to tell me something about the nature of time. Either that, or the nature of love. Both, really. That love can't be measured by the clock of the body. The clock of his—and, one day, my own—dying body. All of us who love one another have always loved and will always love one another. His words are cryptic but deliberate—his eyes are locked on mine, his hold on my fingers adamant, fevered—and I'll return to them in the days and months to come. I'll revisit conversations we've had about Meister Eckhart or Saint John of the Cross, sifting through what I know of mysticism for an antecedent for his message. Some of the happiest evenings of my life have been with my father-in-law, sitting in front of a fire he built (often just to please me, as it wasn't really cold enough to merit one), drinking wine, and talking about things that none of the rest of the family has much interest in. When one of us mentioned a theologian, or began to puzzle over the writings of a favorite mystic, my husband drifted out of the room, his brother picked up the paper, my sister-in-law went to the kitchen to help with dinner. I stayed where I was, on the hearth at the foot of his armchair, my back to the fire.

October 16. A few roses still bloom. He comes home to die in the room that looks out on his trees and his flower beds. It's a sunroom, with big picture windows, and the gold leaves that drop from the maples float down onto the deck just beyond the glass door, every day a new carpet of them to sweep away. With fall's drop in humidity, the light acquires the season's characteristic intensity, and as the branches bare they allow more and more sun to come through them. Sitting with my father-in-law, I am silent and so is he. Sometimes I lay my head next to his. It seems to me that the shorter days are becoming ever brighter, as if they were burning themselves out more quickly.

One evening, when I arrive in Washington, my mother-in-law tells me that earlier that day my father-in-law said he was sick of long faces. He directed her, her sister, and the nurse to stand around his bed and sing, which they did. He told them which songs he wanted—Quaker hymns, mostly, and a few favorite folk songs. "'Tis a Gift to Be Simple." "Michael, Row the Boat Ashore."

With my mother-in-law's sister running the house, and friends bringing in meals, there's no need for me to do any chores when I'm there. Instead, I stay by my father-in-law's bed every minute I can, leaving only to give him privacy with his wife or his brother or one of his sons. More often than not, I'm rubbing his feet. I do it for hours, grateful to be able to provide what feels good to him and communicate my love as words cannot. Every so often, my mother-in-law's sister stands from the dining table and brings me a letter to read aloud. She stacks them on the table as they arrive, and logs each into a ledger, noting both date and sender, about seven hundred so far.

November 8. On the last weekend of my husband's father's life, both my husband and I are with his parents. We've left the younger children at home with a sitter, and brought only our older daughter with us. On Sunday, my husband comes down to breakfast just as the sky is beginning to lighten. He finds me at the foot of his father's bed, eyes closed, rubbing his feet with oil. My husband puts a hand on my shoulder and I open my eyes. "Have you been here all night?" he asks.

"He likes it."

"But you're tired, sweetheart. Take a break. Come have something to eat with me."

"I will. In a minute, I will." I go on rubbing. My father-in-law opens his eyes and smiles at my husband, who comes to take his hand.

"I'm tough competition," he whispers, and my husband bends down to kiss his father's forehead.

We are trying to fill each remaining minute with love. Enough to split time open, to make love run backward and forward. Enough that my father-in-law can feel what he knows: that we've always loved him, and we always will.

January, February, March. In the months after his death, I dream of my father-in-law every night. In the dreams are two of him, one dead, one living. The dead man is in his casket; the other sits among the mourners. I find this unusual, but not impossible, as it would be were I awake. The dreams are crowded with people—family and friends who have come to attend his funeral and who fill a church or an auditorium. One time it's a movie theater with rows of plush red seats; he sits on one side of his wife, with me on the other.

Usually, the dream funerals are bungled. There are not enough pews, or we forget to order food for the reception. We don't give out song sheets, and no one knows the words to the hymns we pick. Each time something goes wrong, all of us are distraught, particularly my mother-in-law, who weeps with frustration. My father-in-law shrugs. Never mind, he tells her. What does it matter?

In one dream, the service takes place at a hunting lodge, and my husband lies down in a fireplace, among the burning logs. He curls himself up in a fetal position, and his legs catch on fire. "Stop him!" I say to my father-in-law, and I grab him by the arm. "Please, don't let him do that!"

Another time, we lose my father-in-law's body; it's been stolen and shipped overseas, where a chemical extracted from his tumors will be used to treat other sick people. Before we can have a funeral, we must get it back. My father-in-law paces in this dream, and I worry that he's growing impatient. I know he can't linger forever in hopes of a funeral that doesn't go awry.

And he doesn't. There's a huge picnic, a family reunion, in a place I've never been, grassy and pleasant. I walk among the people drinking and eating and talking together, but I can't find him. Just as I begin to cry, a phone booth appears, and the phone begins to ring. "Please don't," he says, when I answer. "I don't want you to cry."

True Crime

MARCH 20, 1987. IT STARTED OFF AS A JOKE. HAVING GUESSED I'd never seen such a magazine before, my future husband included an issue of *Startling Detective* among my birthday presents. We'd met a year earlier, both of us enrolled in the University of Iowa's Writers' Workshop, and had been living together for six months. As MFA students, we gathered with our peers to critique one another's short stories; we argued the merits of experimental fiction and the boundaries of magical realism; we hunted down unreliable narrators and used the words *epiphany* and *redemption* whenever the opportunity presented itself. We did not consider hard-boiled, artless accounts of rape and murder a legitimate form of narrative. As reading material it qualified as slumming.

"I knew you'd like it," he said.

"No," I said, bouncing up from our thrift-shop couch, "I *love* it."

The pandering sensationalism; the preponderance of lurid

clichés; prose that had passed from bad to execrable without stopping at worse: He'd found the perfect antidote for the hours I spent rearranging the order of sentences that had themselves required hours in the making. "Oregon's Copycat Sex Murders" was the lead article for March. In the back were ads for handguns, wigs, diet aids, miracle cures, girdles, and correspondence courses to improve your sex life or learn to become a private eye in your own home.

My future husband, who'd imagined the gift as a onetime gag, thought it was funny that I liked what was unarguably pulp, with standards lower than a tabloid's.

After we'd graduated and were packing for a move east, to New York, I was surprised by how many detective magazines I found lying around our living room, jammed between sofa cushions, buried in piles of newspapers. He'd bought a few more, and I'd bought some myself. While the joke of their abysmal prose had worn off, I remained captive to what was irredeemably vulgar and misogynistic. *True Detective, Startling Detective, Front Page Detective*—they were all the same. Whether the bombshell on the cover was hog-tied and gagged by a murderous lothario or luring an innocent man to his death, she was usually wearing no more than lingerie or a bikini. Sex and death: The two were inextricably bound.

The transition from a small Midwestern college town to New York City was predictably vertiginous. Neither of us had lived there before, at least not as an adult working a day job while writing on evenings and weekends. For the first time in my life, I didn't have time to squander on what had been, I decided, a sophomoric attraction to kitsch, the literary equivalent of a pink plastic flamingo jabbed into a patch of lawn.

A decade disappeared before I gave detective magazines another thought—we'd married by then and started a family. I suspect I may have been the only mother in my neighborhood Barnes & Noble to leave her children within the safe embrace of the "Jr." section so she could troll the true-crime shelves while they made their way through *Frog and Toad Together.* I didn't care about murders of practicality undertaken to dispatch an inconvenient spouse or hasten an inheritance. I wanted to read about lust murder, the kind committed by an apparently ordinary man who secretly hunts a girl down, uses her sexually, kills her, discards her lifeless body, and seamlessly reenters his upstanding, workaday life.

Why didn't the familiar plot bore me? I wondered as I glanced up to make sure my children hadn't wandered off while I looked for books I'd be embarrassed to be caught purchasing. If I judged myself by their covers, it wasn't only because they advertised my poor taste in reading material. It was my appetite for true stories of dead girls and their killers that made me uncomfortable. I had a dozen or more dog-eared paperbacks hidden in a cardboard box under my side of the bed. Ted Bundy, Gary Ridgway, Richard Ramirez. I read books about men in whom lust and violence were fused, predators satisfied by nothing less than a girl's halted heartbeat, and I read them at bedtime, using a finger to keep my place in the photo insert so I could flip back and forth between the text and the pictures. The best inserts juxtaposed a victim's high school graduation portrait—or, if she'd been a prostitute, a booking photo—with that of her lifeless, often mutilated body.

At which I stared as if I'd known the dead girl personally and was trying to understand what didn't seem possible—that life had continued without her.

My husband was right. I did bump into things more often than other people. I closed drawers on my fingers, cut myself on can lids and wineglasses I broke in the sink, fell down the stairs, fell up the stairs, and burned myself while cooking. I never hung a picture without hammering a finger along with the nail, and I stubbed my toes almost as soon as I took my shoes off. I forgot to look both ways when I crossed the street; even a collision with a bike messenger and the resulting concussion didn't help me remember. To reach a high ceiling bulb, I climbed a Seussian tower of two dining chairs supporting a stepstool, on top of which was a milk crate. But not if there was anyone home to see.

Didn't I realize I was punishing myself? my husband asked me. Once he sensed intent behind what I believed was accidental, he began to challenge my insistence that I was just clumsy, that was all. After years by my side, he saw what I could not. There were only so many ways of mining my comfortable married life for penance.

And what about all the hours spent reading stories of violated and murdered girls, girls guilty of nothing other than trust? Was that a punitive exercise as well? That the spell these stories cast had never forced me to admit I couldn't—or, as my analyst might have said, wouldn't—let go of the lust-murder plot. How many sickening photo inserts did I have to examine before I made the connection between forensic photographs of female corpses and photographs I persuaded my father to take of me when I was a college girl?

The first thing to happen in a lust murder is that someone finds a girl's body. A janitor lugs trash to the Dumpster and sees her propped against its side, her legs spread wide so everyone will know what got her into this mess. Or the killer drives the dead girl out of town and into the wild, and a deer hunter stumbles over a foot sticking out from a brush-covered berm. If it's a fisherman, he sees her hair first, and how it streams from her head, animate under the water. Soon patrol officers are busy securing the scene, grid-searching the terrain, looking for tire tracks, footprints, torn pantyhose, anything that might speak for a girl who can no longer speak for herself.

She's naked, because the killer strips his victim. One step short of skinning her alive, is how he sees it. Sometimes he needs more and has to dismantle her for a trophy: a finger, a kidney, a nipple.

Or maybe he takes her apart for the sheer pleasure of destruction, of going on living after he's watched the blood run out of her veins.

My father hadn't liked the idea. But for once it was I who manipulated him, suggesting that if he didn't take the occasional picture that I staged, I might not obey his directions the next time he posed me for the ones he wanted.

My father and I never spoke of what it might mean that I insisted on posing before him as a corpse, again and again: the victim of a car crash, a fall, an assault. I didn't plan the pictures ahead of time. They were incidental, the result of my happening upon a usable prop or scene. From the vantage of thirty years, it seems incredible that neither my father nor I acknowledged the meaning of our collaboration. We were always so quick to analyze things—books, movies—eager to excavate meaning from paintings, from the work of other photographers.

Maybe the camera itself obscured his vision. He aimed and shot at a subject already dead. I'd say I'd been playing dead had the message been more artful and less desperate.

"Look at me, Father, now that I've given you what you asked."

Look at what we have done.

The medical examiner arrives on the crime scene and ducks under the yellow tape. He takes the dead girl's temperature to estimate the hour of her death and looks at her wounds to see if they've bled, or didn't bleed because she was already dead when he stabbed her. Or the killer has left bruises in the shape of his hands squeezing her neck, and tiny capillaries burst, and bled into the whites of her blind eyes, telling the ME she was choked. Back at the forensics lab, a broken hyoid bone will confirm strangulation as the cause of death. Before the examiner bags the whole of her, he bags each of the dead girl's hands to preserve what evidence might remain under her nails, perhaps a few of her murderer's skin cells with the signature of his DNA to feed into a national database of genetic profiles.

The examiner will know more when he has her body where he can cut it open. Then he'll see what she had for dinner or if she was already dead when her murderer drowned her. As much as the homicide detective wants the killer's skin cells, he doesn't want the dead girl to have fought for them. He wants to tell her family he has evidence that it had been fast, and if not fast, then insensate. That the killer had drugged her before he mauled and raped her, or that she'd missed being mauled and raped because he'd slit her throat beforehand. Anything was better than a torn fingernail, evidence of a struggle.

"Fuck you," I said. I don't remember why. We were at Bright Angel Point, on the Grand Canyon's North Rim. "I keep hoping," my father said. I don't know what happened next. I held him off for months before I let him have what he wanted, afraid of losing what he called love. But I always lay inert, like a corpse, so he'd know I hadn't given my body to him, only let him take it.

What point was there in running away, he said, when I'd never find anyone who would tolerate what he'd made of me? I wasn't five or ten or fifteen. I was twenty, old enough to condemn and forever bar myself from huddling among the innocent.

That was the way it was with mistakes, my father said when I told him how unhappy I was, how lonely. You never knew how expensive they'd turn out to be.

No. Mostly you didn't know you were making one until it was too late. My mother's parents thought they'd done my father a favor by releasing him from his shotgun marriage to their daughter. As long as he'd go away and not come back, they'd relieve him of responsibilities he couldn't shoulder and payments he couldn't make—alimony, child support. They reassured each other that a boy of eighteen didn't have to start over; he'd yet to begin.

My grandparents steeled themselves to my teenage father's

humiliation at having his wife and firstborn taken from him. They didn't foresee that so grave an insult to his manhood would warp the person he became; they failed to imagine the magnitude of his pride or how, over years, it would inspire a rage that demanded retaliation.

Neither they nor my mostly absent young mother nor I recognized the girl I became, the one who would do anything for what anyone called love. The only person who saw her was my father.

If the dead girl whose story I'm reading isn't a prostitute, she's a college girl out on a hike, or a waitress who went home with the wrong customer. She's been missing long enough that her roommate is frantic, her family more so. If she's not a prostitute, the media invite the missing girl's parents to appear on the nightly news and plead for their daughter's abductor to return her. They have to assume he's capable of remorse, of possessing emotions that resemble their own. They can't understand what makes him who he is, and they don't want to believe such people exist. Her friends stand at intersections handing out flyers printed with her picture over the word REWARD.

I didn't think it was particularly odd to keep a box of lust murders under the bed until I tried to move them to a better spot. What mother would leave books like that lying around where her children might come upon them? I carried them up and down the stairs looking for a place to tuck them away, out of sight, and ended up putting them back under the bed. I did this two or three times, enough to feel self-conscious. Did I want them near me as I slept, and if I did, why? Acknowledging them as bedtime stories gave me more reason to hide them away.

Perhaps I was, as my analyst said, polluted only insofar as I believed myself to be. But what informed my beliefs other than the books I'd read? I'd never taken a sex-ed class; I knew little enough about normal sex, let alone deviance. But Sophocles knew the wages of incest, of pollution that can't be contained. When Oedipus understands that he is responsible for his people's misfortunes—their blighted fields and flocks, famine, plague, infertility—he puts out his own eyes. In *Paradise Lost,* Death is born when Satan beds his own daughter. Dick Diver met his mad wife, Nicole, in the Swiss asylum where he treated her; by the end of *Tender Is the Night,* he's lost his soul to the father who raped her. I was still a bluestocking, with a bluestocking's library. Whose opinion would I hold above Sophocles'?

My favorite of the pictures, and the last we made together, is bloodless. I'm wearing a black dress with a prim white collar and holding a white rose. Eyes closed, I'm lying in a casket I nagged my father to ask an undertaker friend to lend him, a floor model. I thought it might be scary, climbing into a coffin and lying down, especially when the bottom half of the lid was lowered over my legs, but it wasn't—not really. Not when I thought of myself as dead anyway, a body abandoned by its owner. I considered what means there were to rectify my predicament. The closest at hand was my father's revolver, the Colt .357 Magnum he taught me to load and fire. "That's what police use," he said as he watched my hand drop under the unfamiliar weight of a firearm.

—————

Who can interview a dead girl? If a reader is to understand how it happened, this thing so terrible that people can't imagine it for themselves, someone has to re-create her final hours. Maybe there's a girl who got away, and she tells the homicide detective what the killer did before she escaped. She shouldn't have been walking alone on that stretch of road; she knew that. But her car broke down, or a pickpocket stole her wallet, or she spent her bus fare on something else. The lust murderer posed as an officer of the peace, or a night watchman: a big man whose job it is to protect the vulnerable. He seemed nice at first, she tells the detective.

Whoever she was, the girl who got away had been careless, just like the ones who weren't so lucky. Everything would have turned out differently if she had been a better judge of character, or if she hadn't been so headstrong as to hike alone where no one could hear her screams. The prostitute would still be alive if she hadn't been so desperate for a fix that she ignored the killer's eyes and got into his van. If you read enough lust murders, it's clear how vigilant a girl has to be.

Every day for a week I visited the gun on the shelf above my father's suits; sometimes I touched it, and sometimes I just looked. Once, I loaded it. I dropped a single bullet into one of the revolver's six chambers. Wadcutters were the kind of ammunition my father bought, bullets with hollow points that explode to maximize tissue damage. I was with him when he made the purchase. Crime stoppers, I thought when he handed me the little box, heavy as a brick. A bullet would be too fast for regret, but I was afraid of misfiring, and even more than that, I was afraid of myself. On my last visit to the revolver, I looked up from where it was lying in my lap and by chance caught my reflection in the closet's mirrored door. We regarded each other, I and the girl who'd given up all she had to keep the father she'd lost once before. How long had it been since she'd taken off the gold cross she used to wear? She didn't want anyone to mistake her for a decent Christian. I pointed the gun at the girl in the mirror and saw something beyond or beneath her willingness to be debased. Like her father, she was proud.

Whatever part of me I hadn't lost or strangled was the one recording what happened. I knew better than to end such a story on so obvious a metaphor as her incestuous father's pistol.

I put the gun back on the shelf and let what was left of me live.

A dream recurs, a dream that consists of one moment. As if I were watching from the other side of a double mirror, I see myself sitting alone in a small, windowless room painted white, empty aside from the chair beneath me. The room has a single door, and my father is on the other side. I sit facing the door, and I watch the doorknob.

Nothing happens. I wait, that's all. I'm nineteen; soon I'll be twenty. I know it's only a matter of time before the knob turns, the door opens, and my father steps through. I know what future lies ahead, and I know there's no way to escape it.

The only way to get away from my father, the only way I knew, was to leave her behind, the girl he stalked and stole, the one in the college yearbook, the one in that room. She was stupid about love, that girl, and she never knew when people were lying to her.

I kept a few things. Her christening dress, a pair of her baby shoes bronzed into bookends, and a banker's box full of high school notebooks and term papers, all of them typed on onion-skin paper, without a single mistake, the result of watching her fingers on the keys. "What I Am; What I Hope to Become." It was an assignment, so she'd taken it seriously: She did her best to sum herself up. Ten pages held together with a heart-shaped clip: I skimmed them to see what she thought she knew about herself when she was sixteen. That she loved animals and wanted to be a veterinarian? That maybe she'd work for a zoo, taking care of the big cats? She'd gotten an A, of course; she always got A's. She was a slave to praise.

I kept the stuffed dog she'd had all her life and had taken with her to college, and I kept her books, too, a few cartons' worth. To open a volume was to summon the girl who'd licked the gummed bookplate bearing her name and solemnly set it in place. Ex libris. Her grandfather had built her a bookcase and painted it white, and she slept just an arm's length from it. The lamp on her bedside table had a ceramic stand painted with a nosegay of pink flowers, and she scorched a lot of T-shirts by dropping them over its shade to stop light from leaking under her door past bedtime and giving her away.

The door in the dream has no lock, and the room is so small and so empty, the girl so alone. How was it—how could it have been—that I didn't know the cost of failing to protect her? She'd want books, the girl I'd abandoned; she always did, and maybe it would help her to see the story's end.

A single strand of pale hair caught on a thorn, lifting in the air and gleaming for a moment in the sun. Don't miss it. If you're a homicide detective, that's how hard you have to look, how closely you must pay attention and never allow your focus to waver. Otherwise you might mistake it for something it's not—a single filament, say, from a spider's torn web. You have to look closely, because there isn't always a body to find. Sometimes it was long ago that she died, as much as thirty years, and all that's left are her exhumed remains. Other times there isn't even that much. But you don't stop looking. You can't stop looking. Your job is to find what other people refuse to see. By day you hunt for clues, by night assemble them into a map.

You detect her, the dead girl, no matter if you have to use a magnet to stir a hundred woodstoves' worth of cold ashes to find a single eyelet from her sneaker. Not everything burns away. A girl can be killed, but not obliterated. And even one tiny eyelet is something. Something for the mourners to bury.

Holiday Lies

By NIGHTFALL, THE FIRE WOULD BE BELCHING SPARKS ONTO THE beige rug. We'd have to let it die down to coals before roasting chestnuts. Along the front of the mantel, my grandfather has stretched fine wires on which to hang greeting cards. The mantel itself is covered with candles molded into Santas, snowmen, and choirboys, all placed with care among miniature flocked fir trees and garlands of imitation holly and poinsettia. Having never been lit, the candles' wicks are flattened down into their soft heads, the black paint on Santa's boots and belt chipping from long wear, the red of his suit thinning to expose the uncolored wax below. Once, the Santa candles were identical but, stooped under lumpy sacks of toys, they fall over a lot, and not one stands back up looking as he did before.

The living room is warm, a balmy eighty-five or so. Sun streams through the windows and casts glowing white lozenges on the carpet, hot enough that the cats avoid rather than seek them out. Outside, roses are blooming and the neighbor boys are shirtless, gripping new skateboards with bare toes. It's December in Southern California. I'm wearing a wool dress and black patent-leather Mary Janes, melting, just like the wax Santas, and trying to hold still while my grandfather fiddles with his camera. When it's dark he'll plug in the lights strung under the eaves and around the fir trees along the driveway. A wreath the size of a truck tire eclipses the door knocker as well as the knob; mistletoe dangles from a red ribbon in the foyer. To avoid what strikes me as a sanctioned demand for a kiss from anyone who might come calling, I take the doorbell's chime as my cue to run upstairs.

My grandparents fetishize Christmas. Probably there are other families who sit down to a holiday meal inspired by Dickens's *A Christmas Carol,* although I don't imagine many of them anticipate the arrival of a hamper from Fortnum & Mason, in London, to announce the season. Not in Los Angeles in the 1960s. Under the hamper's lid are a York ham, Scottish smoked salmon, jars of real mincemeat (made with suet), and the culmination of our holiday dinner: a three-pound plum pudding immediately whisked away and elevated to a high perch, where it will remain until its unveiling, its days numbered, just like the little windows on my Advent calendar.

Prawns with cocktail sauce, turkey with stuffing, mince pies, roasted potatoes and carrots and onions: We're always too full for dessert by the time my grandmother turns off the lights, retrieves the brandy-soaked pudding from the sideboard, and places it before my grandfather. I watch as he sets a lit match to its glistening brown flank, conjuring a wreath of blue flames that dance around the sprig of holly resting on top. The lights go back on, my grandfather dismantles the pudding; my grandmother tops each slab with a dollop of hard sauce and serves it on the Christmas china. My grandparents are elderly European Jews raised in Orthodox homes, but we don't keep separate sets of plates in a kosher kitchen. Instead we have two sets of Christmas plates, twelve of the red-rimmed Spode with a Christmas tree in the center for dinner with our extended family on Christmas Eve, and six of the everyday Johnson Brothers, whose painted yuletide scene mirrors our own holiday decor. The everyday set has mugs and bowls, as well. We use them for all of December, and on into January. On Twelfth Night both sets are packed away until the following Advent season.

As a child, I don't know what differentiates a menorah from a candelabra or a dreidel from a plain old spinning top; the gelt coins in my stocking are embossed with busts of smiling reindeer. I'll be in college before I understand our family pageant as a celebration not of Advent but of assimilation. My grandparents left Judaism in an old world they'd forsaken, buried with the relatives they lost during the Holocaust. Chanukah, like Kristallnacht, is a word I never hear at home.

But I know all about Boxing Day, when we have an open house, the dining table's Christmas centerpiece—a Santa in a sleigh pulled by gold-antlered reindeer—competing for space with a punch bowl of eggnog, as well as fruitcake, ham and potato pie, smoked salmon, and Christmas tree cookies sparkling with green sugar crystals. It's London, circa 1910, because my grandparents' Gentile fantasies are retroactive, reaching back to thoroughly flock if not whitewash their own childhoods.

The college girl I become will want to fault her grandparents for their embrace of the season. But if sophomoric political correctness suggests defining their December pageant as evidence of self-loathing, it also requires forgetting for whom the illusion is staged. My mother's parents may not be Christian but they have a Christmas wish: that my mother and I never regard ourselves as targets for the anti-Semitism they discovered everywhere they'd lived, including California. Even as America was at war with Nazi Germany, my grandparents were barred from living where they wanted. "No point in making a bid on that house," the real estate agent told them—not with British passports that classified them as "Hebrew." Not with a surname taken from one of the twelve tribes of Israel. "No Jews in that community." The prejudice they endured wasn't dangerous, but it was real. The day my grandmother heard a parking attendant call her beloved baby blue Cadillac a "Jew canoe" was the day before she traded it in for a Lincoln.

Tinsel and holly and waiting in line to sit on a department-store Santa's red velvet lap, the spangled tree that remains in the sunroom through twelfth night: For as long as I live in my grandparents' home, the glittering spell they cast works. I'll have grown up and moved out before I have any notion of myself as a Jew. In fact, having been the enthusiastic object of my grandparents' Christmas spell, I'll have held tight to childhood fantasies my friends have long ago shucked off.

So tight, perhaps, that a vestige of enchantment remains. At twelve, my younger daughter, whose observations often startle me for their precocity, claims she still believes in Santa Claus. Is it even possible, I wonder, to navigate middle school and preserve such a faith intact? And if, somehow, she has, what good could come from my destroying what she's worked to protect?

"Don't you?" she challenges me. I'm not sure who's performing for whom, and taking the time to formulate a cleverly ambiguous answer would tip her off. And, really, what's the harm?

"Of course I do," I say.

Setting out the cookies, pouring the cocoa, reading "The Night Before Christmas": For years, my husband and I stirred all three children into a frenzy of anticipation so intense they couldn't fall asleep. At three o'clock on Christmas morning they'd trample us in our bed, chattering and squealing and pointing out the window at the spot in the sky where they'd seen a reindeer-drawn sleigh streak past the stars. We never suggested Santa wasn't real; we left it up to other children. The girls survived without sustaining observable trauma, but one day our middle child, the boy, came home from school in a wild rage. "Why didn't you tell me!" he said, and I think he even stamped his feet as he described the humiliation of his playground contretemps. Taunted by classmates, he understood with a sudden and terrible certainty that they were right. There was no Santa Claus; he was indeed a "big baby"; I had betrayed him by not arming him with the truth.

The youngest, having been given one after another reason to doubt Santa Claus's existence, will not let him go, even as she approaches her teenage years. "Is Santa real?" she asks after overhearing an older girl reminisce about Christmases back when she believed.

"I guess some people don't think so," I lie carefully, still chastened by the misery I caused her brother. "But I do." She says nothing, and her silence communicates my failure to answer the question. "I mean," I try again, "it's a little like it is with God. Some people do, some don't."

"I don't," she says, about God.

"Are you sure?" I say.

"What's it called when you aren't sure?"

"Agnostic?"

"Can you be that about Santa?"

"Of course." I tell her the story of herself and the Tooth Fairy, one I know she enjoys.

When she was about five, our younger daughter discovered the little silver box in my study, the one that held baby teeth I'd exchanged for little gifts or, when I had them, silver dollars. I never felt a fairy should use everyday currency.

"Why do you have these?" she asked.

"I'm the Tooth Fairy," I said, and she laughed delightedly at the ridiculous idea of her mother, solid and earthbound, as a fairy.

We repeated the dialogue, many times. She picked up the box, asked why I collected baby teeth, and laughed at my answer. Until the day she didn't. "Oh," she said. "Oh no. You really are the Tooth Fairy. You were telling the truth. All the time you were telling the truth."

She cried, and I took her on my lap and told her a Tooth Fairy story about her much older sister. One night, when I slipped into her sister's bedroom to exchange tooth for coin, I woke her up while groping under her pillow. I was sure she'd seen me, but I retreated into a shadow until she turned her face to the wall and fell back asleep. Then I took the tooth and left the little present. In the morning she called me to her room.

"Look," she said. "Look what the Tooth Fairy gave me." I

examined the tiny pink satin purse with a golden Sacagawea dollar inside. "Is it real?" she asked about the coin, one she'd never seen before.

"I think so. I wonder where the Tooth Fairy finds things like this," I said of the tiny purse.

"I don't know. But, Mom, listen. I saw her. I saw the Tooth Fairy. Last night."

"Really?"

"Yes! And you know what?" She looked me up and down, the whole of me. "She isn't at all how I thought. She's—she's as big as you! And you know what else?"

"What?"

"She didn't fly in the window. I don't think she even has wings because she walked into my room, just like you do." I nodded, waiting for the punch line, my Tooth Fairy days over. But they weren't. "Isn't that amazing, Mom? Isn't it? I just— I never would have guessed a fairy could be so tall."

My daughter smiled and showed me her missing tooth. Eight years old, old enough to know better, she closed her fingers over the bright coin in her palm.

The Couch Account

ON THE DAY SHE DISCOVERS SHE CAN NO LONGER WALK OR EVEN stand without assistance, my mother orders seventeen pairs of shoes, one pair at a time, from various catalogues spread over her bed. Neiman Marcus, Saks Fifth Avenue, Bonwit Teller. Forty-two years old, her bones crumbling from cancer that has metastasized from her breast, she is a no-longer-beautiful woman whose vanity has nothing on which to fix other than her size 7AA feet, the only part of her withered body that disease hasn't marred but actually enhanced. Because we keep the bedclothes off her feet—lest the pressure of blankets contort them, curling the toes over, as they would otherwise, or the sheet rub and irritate their skin—my mother's delicate, pampered toes are always directly in her line of sight. While she is bedridden, her feet become softer, paler, and more slender, kept immaculately pedicured by an indulgent visiting nurse.

It turns into a days-long spree. It's 1985—there's no Jimmy Choo or Manolo Blahnik. Instead it's Maud Frizon, Charles

Jourdan, Ferragamo, Yves Saint Laurent, Pappagallo, Chanel, Etienne Aigner, Bally, Christian Dior. Eighty-eight pairs of shoes are stacked on the shelves of her walk-in closet, most in their original boxes, and she's on the phone buying more.

My mother's partner and I stand together in their small kitchen, eavesdropping on her conversations with telephone salespeople.

"You have the matte black, but not the patent leather, or you don't have either in that size?" My mother enjoys opportunities to allude to her Cinderella feet, just as she does calling attention to mine, which belong to an ugly stepsister who must chop off her toes to fit into a glass slipper.

"You have to take it away from her," I whisper, referring to his credit card, on which she's charging all these shoes she'll never wear.

He shakes his head. "I can't," he says. He's a gentle man, soft-spoken. An alcoholic, he drinks steadily all day without ever descending into perceivable drunkenness. Like me, he avoids conflict. For eleven years, he and my mother live together while he remains married to a fanatical Catholic who refuses to divorce him, just as he refuses to initiate proceedings against her.

"Please," I say. "It's your card. She's spending thousands of dollars."

"We'll return them," he says.

There's a window between the kitchen and the room in which we set up my mother's hospital bed, an opening presumably through which to pass dishes of food, although no one has ever used it for that purpose. The two of us stand at that small window, its shutters closed, watching through the wooden slats. My mother looks almost happy, or even purely happy. What she's doing isn't a symptom of desperation or panic. Those are my feelings. Maybe they had been hers before she obliterated them with a volley of shoes, and, in doing so, transferred them to me.

The UPS man brings the shoes to the door, and we sign for the packages and stack them on the table in the hall. My mother, confined to her hospital bed, never inquires about all the orders that appear not to have been filled. Shoes continue to arrive after her death, and I open the boxes and complete the forms necessary to return them, printing the words "purchaser deceased" in the space provided for the reason for their rejection. I wait until there are two or three pairs before I take them to the post office; I could wait a day longer, but I can't stand seeing them on the table, not so many at a time, so I stand in line with two or three boxes, giving me plenty of time to think about what I'm holding in my arms.

Days spent squandering money she didn't have on shoes she couldn't wear: the perfect coda to my mother's short life. For as long as I'd known her she'd been spending with a vengeance. Not just spending irresponsibly, although she was irresponsible, but spending money with the intent to punish her mother. By the time I could identify the arena of their conflict, my mother and grandmother were practiced adversaries, performing an indefinite object lesson in the disparate misuses of money.

Offered as love, and withheld as punishment. Dangled as bait. Bestowed in company. Withdrawn in secret. It could be made to seem plentiful, as plentiful as water—which, my

grandmother said was the way my mother spent it, *like water*—
and, just as suddenly, it could dry up. It could bind one person
to another; just as easily, it could pry them apart.

Our home was always filled with a generalized, ambient
anxiety about money. The only real source of it was my grandmother's trust fund, left to her by her father, a self-made mil-
lionaire. Private worries over money's tendency to seep away,
like air from a tire with a slow leak, did nothing to correct my
mother's profligacy; perhaps it even accelerated it. My grandfather's pension was modest, and he kept his bank account separate from my grandmother's—at her insistence. I know of
incompetent math students who, once a dollar sign is attached
to a number, suddenly understand calculations that had previously confounded them, numbers spread across the firmament,
orderly and beautiful, like the glorious bright embers of fire-
works. For my grandfather, the opposite seems to have been
true. A math prodigy, he had no instinct for commerce. Most
shamefully, he had turned down an opportunity to buy a siz-
able portion of the Las Vegas Strip. This was in 1942; the country was at war; he thought the place was "too vulgar to catch
on." My grandmother never spoke of it, and never forgave him
for it. When I was a child, in the sixties, there were household
expenses he assumed, the gas bill, the gardener, and others that
she did, like the cost of the house itself.

My mother was twenty-four when she lived on her own for the
first time, trying and failing to escape my grandmother, who
had bullied her into divorcing my father. But years passed, my
mother found herself alone, with no husband and her child
cared and provided for by her parents, and she still didn't have

money for what she wanted. She worked as a legal secretary, but she didn't earn enough to rent the apartment or buy furniture she liked; she couldn't drive a white Mercedes 380SL; she couldn't afford to have someone clean the apartment she didn't like.

But she did have a means of extracting restitution, and she had accomplices. Lanvin and Sonia Rykiel. Ungaro, Dior, and Yves Saint Laurent. Schiaparelli. The bills she ran up were worse than staggering; my grandmother learned to sit down before opening them. My mother saved me her bags from Bonwit Teller, white shopping bags painted with nosegays of violets. I didn't use them. I kept them folded flat on a high shelf in my closet. Pristine, they looked new, unused. She shopped for food anywhere my grandmother ran a tab—the grocer, the butcher, the bakery. I rarely stood with her at a register when she didn't say, "Put it on the account, please." My grandmother gave my mother duplicates of all her credit cards, and told her not to use them. They were, she said, for "emergencies."

Even as a child I understood how perverse this was, akin to Bluebeard's handing his new young bride the key to the locked chamber that held the corpses of her butchered predecessors. For my mother, not having a pair of shoes she loved *was* an emergency. Did my grandmother want my mother to use the cards so that when the bills arrived she had a reason to initiate a fight? Was my mother the child my grandmother intended her to be, the one who would never grow up and leave her, who would always understand the terms of her imprisonment?

I was with my mother when she discovered that the I. Magnin account had been terminated. I was leaning against a warmly lit glass counter, looking at the scarves displayed within. Pucci, silk printed with arabesques of vivid pinks and greens, red purple blue, roller coasters of color. I was plunging my eyes up and down a particularly vertiginous sweep of hot pink, doing it over and over to see if I could summon the nausea of a real roller coaster's plunge, when I heard the saleslady say she was sorry, the card hadn't been accepted. Perhaps my mother would like to pay another way? I looked up and saw her pale, manicured fingers accept the defunct credit card, its shiny surface embossed with my grandmother's name, and slip it back into her black wallet with the gold interlocking C's. Her face was invisible from my vantage point at the counter's edge, but I could see her white neck color with embarrassment.

My mother pulled her car door closed with enough force to confirm what I dreaded. I felt sick even before we were headed for Coldwater Canyon in a car accelerating in tandem with my mother's anger. I figured I had, at best, five hairpin turns before I had to ask her to pull over, which elicited disgust more often than sympathy. It turned out to be only two. Or maybe it was twice that she pulled over. I do remember vomiting on my grandparents' driveway, because it splashed the hubcap of my mother's car and I had to hose it and the driveway off.

Inside the house, tears and remonstrations: How could my grandmother have put my mother in such a position, humiliate her like that? How, my grandmother countered, could my mother put *her* in such a position, forcing her to close an account by buying things she didn't need, running up bills my grandmother couldn't pay? Their fights turned ugly, but they never betrayed their catalyst. My mother never said it out loud. She wasn't brave enough to tell her mother that I wasn't the only person she blamed for ruining her life.

———

In college, I shared stories of my mother's sprees with my boy-friend. I wanted him to know who my mother was, and I wanted him to dislike her—to understand our tortured rela-tionship. My grandmother had two trust funds, I explained to him. One had been set up for her by her father and was irrevo-cable. The income was hers but she couldn't touch the princi-pal, which would pass to my mother after her death. To me, my grandmother had willed an identical trust fund, which she had inherited at her sister's death, so it was no longer irrevocable; this was the money my grandmother was whittling away to pay my mother's rent, buy her a car (a Toyota Corolla, the least expensive car on the market at the time), to make her loans she would never repay. My boyfriend was angry. He looked at me in my thrift-store sweater and used army-surplus pants and re-minded me that my inheritance was half gone, but that wasn't what I cared about. In protest against my mother's extrava-gance, as a means of accusing her, I spent as little as I could on clothes. I was doing as I would do for many years, for all the years it took before I forgave my mother: I was making myself into her antithesis, and announcing it. Wearing what she wouldn't wear, getting my hair cut for free at a beauty school, my cavities filled for free at the dental school. Both were un-fortunate decisions, but at least hair goes on growing.

"That is totally selfish and unfair. Criminally selfish!" My boyfriend paced and waved his arms around. "You're going to confront her," he told me. "This Christmas, when you're home for break, you're going to tell her that she can't spend your money. It's your money. Security for you."

"No," I said. "It isn't mine, not really, not yet. And anyway I wouldn't do that. It's not the kind of thing I'd do." In fact, I couldn't imagine myself saying such a thing. I'd been taught never to talk about money, because, like talking about sex and politics, it was vulgar; like religion, it was private. But day after night after day, my boyfriend harangued me. I was passive, he said. I was subservient. I always let my mother have her way. Everyone did. No one ever held her accountable for anything. I'd never grow up, I'd never have a life, I'd always be a child if I didn't confront her. Did I want to be a child forever?

I didn't, no. I'd seen what that was like. I promised to confront her, and I did. Generally, the hostility between my mother and me was not articulated but acted out. Instead of telling me I was fat (I wasn't), she gave me clothes a size or more too small. "Oh," she'd say, when she'd coaxed me into trying on whatever it was, and she'd turn me around to see every seam strain. "Oh, I didn't realize you were that big." She never said I was ugly; instead she offered me a nose job for my sixteenth birthday, a gift I didn't accept. But this time, when I raised the issue, my mother attacked me straight on, stepping toward me until she was only inches away.

"You," she said. "No one owes you anything. Do you understand that? Do you?"

"I . . . I didn't—"

"Nothing. Nothing. You don't deserve a thing. How dare you suggest that my mother's money—*my mother's*—might be yours?"

"I didn't mean—"

"I know exactly what you meant. And you're wrong."

I wish I could remember the end of the fight. I know I was frightened and very sorry I'd let my boyfriend convince me to voice what had been his worry alone. And I was shocked that all the things he'd said about my mother—that she was uncaring and jealous and destructive—seemed to be true. I'd defended her to him. I'd said she was thoughtless, not mercenary, but I was, I guess, wrong.

In the end, what remained of the trust fund I was to inherit was spent on medical bills, as my mother was uninsured when given the diagnosis of breast cancer. She'd taken the money my grand-mother gave her for health insurance premiums and spent it on something else. Something that made her feel safer, perhaps, more properly armored than insurance ever could. Shoes, I imagine, beautiful shoes made by Maud Frizon. I remember the dove-gray pair I admired most of all, but none of her shoes fit my feet. When she died we gave her shoes away, most of them to the home-health aide they fit. What the aide didn't want went to Goodwill.

"Separate bank accounts!" This was the single piece of advice my grandmother gave me before I married.

"But why?" I asked. "We're sleeping in the same bed. Why can't our money be together?"

She gave me a look I'd seen before, one intended to remind the graduate student I was at the time that there was little of practical value to be learned in school.

"What if you want to clear out in a hurry?" she said. "Then what?"

"Oh, come on, Nana. I can't get married with an exit strategy."

"Of course you can! That's what those, those what-do-you-call-thems are."

"Prenups?"

She nodded vigorously, all four feet, eleven inches of her.

"I think we feel differently about this. I don't think there's much point in having this conversation. We'll just end up arguing."

"You mark my words," she said.

I grow inured to the line in the post office, inured to what seems the staff's purposeful lethargy. Or maybe I like having to wait as long as I do, with my arms holding tight to boxes of wishes, wishes destined to go unfulfilled, but my mother's wishes nonetheless. The weeks after her death turn into months, the stream of shoes trickles off to only two and then one pair a week, and then they stop arriving altogether. What I complained about looks like less of a chore in hindsight. Already my mother herself has been reduced to boxes, and they in turn grow fewer and fewer as the years pass and I move from one home to the next.

Now there are only two. In one is her handbag, just as it was on the day she died. It's beige leather, crosshatched, with a shoulder strap. Folded on top is one of the scarves she used after she lost her hair. It's rare that I open the bag; when I do I always unfold the scarf to smell it and check that the few fallen hairs remain. Underneath the scarf is a date book, 1985, its pages blank. Tucked between them is a yellow snippet of paper torn from a legal pad bearing my mother's hand: *Nam Myōhō Renge Kyō*, a Nichiren Buddhist chant intended to deliver the chanter into the presence of Buddha and in this way adjust her karma. I don't know how many times one is meant to repeat it, or if she ever said it at all.

There's no wallet, nor any money, in my mother's purse;

what few credit cards she had belonged to either her mother or her partner. A business card from a priest at Loyola Marymount University shares the inner pocket with an emery board and a laminated photograph of a white glowing blob against a cosmic black backdrop that was, my mother told me, the soul of Paramahansa Yogananda. The main compartment holds her "Catholic's Guide," the prayers in Latin as well as English, two pairs of reading glasses (both with frames by Dior), and three scapulars, one with a prayer to the Virgin, standing with the baby Jesus in a circle of prayer, another with Mary on one side and a snippet of the "Hail Mary" on the other. The third bears a promise: "Whosoever dies wearing this scapular shall not suffer eternal fire."

In the purse's single outside pocket is a letter on a piece of my grandfather's stationery. He wrote it a year before he died, two years before she did. With its underscored instructions, it reads as little more than a scolding-before-the-fact, closing with a formulaic promise of undying love. That these are the last words she received from her father, and that she kept them with her until the day she died, will never lose their power to grieve me.

Carole darling,

I am sure you will <u>understand</u> and <u>abide</u> by my wishes as expressed in my will and in my notes to Ralph and Ronnie [my mother's much older half brothers].
My eternal love will always be with you.
God bless you,

Your devoted father

———

My grandmother will have been dead for twenty years by the time I have a bank account separate from the one I share with my husband. I don't open it to "clear out in a hurry," but to keep funds reserved for a research project separate from our shared account.

"Close it," my husband suggests, after the money is spent, the research completed.

"No," I say. "I think I'm going to keep it."

"For what?"

"Oh, I don't know. This and that."

It's the opposite of the kind my grandmother had in mind. It's not a nest egg for the day I might want to bolt, but an account dedicated to the preservation of marriage, or at least marital harmony.

"Can't we get one now, can't I order it?" I ask the question for years. "Please?"

"We'll have to hold out until next month, after the tuition bills are paid," my husband says. After the oil bill, after Christmas, after we've finished paying for that trip to Amsterdam, after the taxes are paid. Who am I to challenge his insistence that no piece of furniture is worth going to debtors' prison? I know the couch will always be triaged to the back of the line.

And so the account discovers its purpose, and takes an eponymous title: the Couch Account. The occasional freelance check small enough not to be missed; a windfall of unexpected royalties (three figures, rarely four—more of a breeze than a wind); reimbursement for travel. I work at home; I get to the mail first; I take and deposit them into the Couch Account. It takes a while, but once it hits the necessary mark, I'm off to

ABC Carpet & Home, a woman with the power to purchase objects whose prices remain hidden, and therefore unchallenged. To avoid trying to justify the profligacy of purchasing jeans that cost 500 percent more than my husband's. To give an extravagant gift without a credit card bill to prove it so. To write a check bearing only my name to replace the mirror I sideswiped off the Volvo up the block. To adjust the discrepancy between how much I thought the lamp cost and what it did cost. Before we celebrate the couch's first anniversary, my separate account has acquired a new name, slurred from the previous one: the "Cancha Count?" or, formally, the "Can't You Count?"

Well, no, not always—it's one of the reasons I have a separate bank account.

The Forest of Memory

As a girl contemplating the mysteries and attractions of independence, of growing up and moving away from home to attend college and then graduate school—moving toward what I believed would be my real, or real*er* life—I never imagined myself entering the world of adults as an *only child*. Wasn't this a state of being that ended, necessarily, with childhood? After all, no one spoke of "only adults." As far as I could tell, unattached adults included the not-yet-married who were looking for love, single mothers or fathers who'd perhaps given up on love, divorcées on the rebound, people confirmed in spinsterhood or bachelordom, and those who had married and were subsequently widowed.

In the wake of her divorce from my father, my mother, once an only child—and still a teenager—was promoted to "single." She had a handful of affairs and, by the time I was ten, had embarked on what would become her last relationship, with a man who remained at her side until the end of her short life. Long before I could articulate it, I understood that the aloneness of adults was measured in terms of romantic coupling. The term for it—the state of being "single"—sounded enough like "singular" to seem desirable to me. Certainly it was a much more attractive word than "only," with its connotations of meagerness, of deprivation, its annoying habit of rhyming with "lonely."

Born in 1961, I was raised among families in which single parents were very much an exception to the nuclear rule. Death, not divorce, was supposed to leave mothers unmarried. Also, almost all the children I knew had at least one brother or sister. The worst part of being an only child, I felt, was the pity it elicited; people assumed I lacked a genuine childhood. Evidently such an undertaking was impossible in the absence of siblings. But a family of seven lived next door to my grandparents, and whenever I liked, I could sample their noise and chaos and petulant squabbling—and then escape when I'd had my fill of what struck me as a more uncomfortably Darwinian existence than my own.

By virtue of being middle-aged, I am no longer an only child. At least I don't call myself one, not any more than I began to identify myself as an orphan at the age of thirty, when I became the single living member of my original family. I have no aunt, uncle, or cousin who is not many times removed from my twig of the family tree. My mother had no full siblings, only two half brothers, adults living in Europe when she was born. My father was gone by the time I turned one. I have become, unarguably, the sole keeper of my history.

Who else would care to preserve my bronzed baby shoes,

my christening dress, or my report cards? Who else inherit my mother's baby teeth, my grandfather's reading glasses, my grandmother's purse—I keep it in the same box with my mother's—and in it her wallet filled with old credit cards, many for businesses that no longer exist)? My great-grandfather's Masonic ring. A silver baby rattle, blackened by tarnish—whose? A tiny Torah scroll wound inside a sterling, filigreed ark, and an antique gold pendant in the form of a swastika, an ancient cosmic symbol that before 1935 had yet to become an object of terror and loathing. Three canes that once belonged to my grandfather (one unscrews to reveal a hidden dagger, the weapon of a gentleman who walked alone, at night, in dangerous cities). A pair of very beautiful hardwood shoe trees (also his). And hundreds of photographs, many of people I no longer recognize, others taken decades before I was born, of relatives I never knew. The entire inventory of my family's "material history," as an anthropologist would call such a collection, belongs to me. It is mine to do with what I will, to make sense of, perhaps, assembling the pieces into a coherent whole, a kind of narrative group portrait complete with background and foreground. Or to make into fiction, to invent a history that is possible, but untrue.

That swastika, to take the most dramatic, and puzzling, example: Where, and from whom, did my Jewish grandmother acquire such an object? Why did she keep it? Her older sister, who lived in Paris, barely survived the Occupation. The gold swastika, hidden away for the shameful thing it has become, upon such a piece of evidence I could begin to fabricate a sinister relative, a diseased branch on the family tree. Like all the contents of those boxes stacked in my basement, the swastika is solid, immutable, unchanging.

But what of my memories, decades old and unavoidably inaccurate? I have no lockbox. Instead, a mind. Not a brain, but whatever it is that animates my brain: a highly permeable assemblage of loves and fears and plans, strengths and frailties, desire and dread and the intent—dimly conscious, at best—to manage all these in service of that slippery entity *me*. Me, as distinct from the rest of humanity. I try honorably to remember things as they really were, but each time, the context in which I revisit a scene from my past—walking through a park, listening as my daughter practices piano—necessarily informs and alters the original. If biology, chemistry, and psychiatry can agree on anything, it is that memories are not received but created. What's more, they're subject to automatic, unavoidable revision. Honor is useless here.

My husband alluded to a mishap he believed he had witnessed. In 1994, our older daughter, then four, and our son, two, stepped into an elevator while I was folding the stroller. I looked up, the doors closed, my children ascended without me. As we were visiting a big apartment building, with a whole bank of elevators, an hour elapsed before a woman who found them in the laundry room reunited the three of us in the lobby.

"You weren't there," I said.

"Yes, I was."

"No, if you'd been with us, if there had been two parents in that situation, it never would have happened."

"But I was sure I was there." He looked at me, confused.

"It's just that we've spoken of what happened enough times that you think you were with us, but you weren't." He nodded slowly, not quite convinced. "We could call Lori," I said. "She'll remember that it was just me and the kids." Lori was

the friend whom I'd taken our children to see, and who en-
listed her doorman and neighbors to help find and return them.

But what of my memories? There is nothing that unfolded in
the house of my childhood that anyone else can confirm, or deny.
Countless transactions, most without consequence, but some
fraught with significance—primal, formative, determining—lack
any witness other than myself. In the abstract, my being free of
siblings, of parents, of anyone who might object or even take
note of an untruth, might provide a tempting invitation to re-
invent history. But only in the abstract, only in theory. When
I test the idea, contemplating how completely possible it is to
rewrite my early years, it frightens me. What I feel isn't free-
dom but a free fall, and what could check the speed of my descent? What we call "reality" depends on its being observed by
at least one person. When a tree falls in my forest of memories
and no one else hears it, has it happened?

To be less philosophical, imagine yourself at a cocktail
party, moving from one clot of guests to the next, one conversation to another. Are not these inadvertent opportunities to
eavesdrop on the self as it slides from one context into another,
shedding some pretenses, picking up others, revealing what,
minutes before, it had hidden, sufficiently disturbing? If identity is fluid under these pedestrian circumstances, how reliable
is the self whose past exists only inside one's own head? How,
without parents or siblings, can I really know what or who I
was?

Among my memories, nothing more material than traces of
neurochemicals in my cerebral cortex, Christmas morning,

1966, has achieved the status of the gold swastika. It is the most puzzling and disturbing of all I possess. I return and return to it, come to it with questions. I woke up early, so early that it was still dark outside. But winter mornings were dark, and I was always up before my grandparents or my mother. I was five years old. I got out of bed; I didn't check the time. Either I couldn't yet read a clock or I was too intent on the stocking that hung from one of my bed's tall posts. My grandparents' house included a hearth that was greeting-card perfect for hanging a Christmas stocking; the mantel was carved from a massive oak beam and outfitted with hooks from which dangled pokers and pincers and bellows, and an antique bed warmer and chestnut roaster, but I was not encouraged to leave my empty stocking in their company. I wonder if this wasn't because a single stocking looked too forlorn there by itself, too *only*.

I stood on the end of my bed to lift the bulging thing from over the post's finial. How satisfying was the stocking's weight and the way tissue-paper wrappings crinkled from within it! This stocking was one I inherited from my mother and had her name, Carole, embroidered across its top. Below was an appliquéd tree of green wool felt, decorated with pea-size ornaments made of colored glass and candles fashioned from minuscule strips of white patent leather, each about the size of half a toothpick, an orange bead for a flame. As if it were still hers, I carried the stocking to my mother's room to unpack its contents with her. With regard to the issue of Santa Claus's identity, I teetered on a cusp between what I wished and what I feared. That it might have been my mother who assembled so perfect an array of tiny gifts, that she could have known me so well, was a more seductive and cherished idea than that of a jolly old man who squeezed down chimneys. In service to

Santa, my grandfather effected the standard transformations, reducing the cookies and cocoa left on the mantel to crumbs and dregs, a thank-you note written in an unfamiliar hand. And he performed a supplementary trick, dipping his shoes into the cold ashes and leaving a trail of footprints from there to my bedroom and back, a trail so convincing that I was afraid it was true. Santa Claus had watched me sleep, he'd touched my bedpost. I didn't mind thinking about him in the living room, near the tree or the fireplace, but I didn't want him in my bedroom.

I wanted the stocking to be my mother's work. I intended to watch her as I unpacked it, in order to gauge her investment in my pleasure. I remember—I can see—my mother's bed, which, as revealed by the moonlight, had not been slept in, and I stood for some minutes holding the stocking and trying to imagine a benign reason for her absence. Was there such a thing? Had I a brother or sister, I would have gone at once to his or her room that we might confer over this unexpected— alarming—turn of events. But I was alone, and so I walked by myself through the hall to the shadowy living room. When I'd determined my mother was nowhere in the house, I went to my grandmother's bedside and touched her shoulder. A light sleeper, she woke instantly and sat forward rather than up from her pillows, piled high to keep her upright and offset the breathlessness caused by her rheumatic heart.

"What?" she said. "What is it?" When I told her, she swung her feet over the side of the bed and stamped one in anger. "If that doesn't—" she began, but didn't finish. Instead she snapped on the light and woke my grandfather. "Gone!" she announced to his startled countenance. "How do you like that! She's gone! Snuck off in the middle of the night!"

Immediately I understood that alerting my grandmother to my mother's disappearance had been the exactly wrong thing to do. My mother wasn't lost—she'd escaped. And I had betrayed her. I, who was always searching for a means of ingratiating myself, of proving my worth to my remote and distracted young mother, of insinuating myself between her and the lovely reflection in her mirror, between her and the novel in her lap, the telephone receiver in her hand. I had just done something awful and irrevocable.

The fight they had later that morning, when my grandmother accused my mother of being a—what word would she have used? Not "slut." Certainly not "whore." Whatever my grandmother did or didn't say, their fight was what my mother ended up calling "the last, last straw, the absolute, final end." "Tart?" Maybe, except "tart" wasn't a word my grandmother used in anger. She thought "tart" was funny. Ditto "trollop." "Promiscuous" was a little clinical for my grandmother's lexicon. "Cheap," I guess. She might have called my mother "cheap" for sneaking out to spend the night with a boyfriend. "Cheap," like other comparatively mild slurs, was a word my grandmother could pronounce as a dire insult. But just as possibly, she might have used no words, she might have just screamed: That was a standard, and unanswerable, strategy. My grandmother's inarticulate, animal howls that seemed to presage madness, or violence, or both, often won her an argument, either because of their inherent power to terrorize or because they testified to her ruthlessness, her stop-at-nothing determination to win.

A month or two later, my mother moved out for good. Unwittingly, I had been the catalyst for my own abandonment. As soon as she was gone, I decided I absolutely did believe in

Santa Claus, and that deep down I had known all along it was he who'd filled the stockings.

The painter René Magritte remembered the suicide of his mother, Régina, as happening in this way. In 1912, Magritte was fourteen. He shared a bedroom with his mother, and one night awoke to find her gone. He roused the rest of the household, and they searched but could find her nowhere inside. But beyond the front door, traces of her steps led to a nearby bridge over the Sambre River, into which the woman had thrown herself. In the middle of the night, René stood on the bank and watched as his mother's corpse was pulled feetfirst from the water, her face covered by her nightdress, her body naked, and luminously white in the moonlight.

Asked what they remembered of the death of Mme. Magritte, René's childhood friends recalled that, though they themselves had all cried in fear and grief, René betrayed no emotion in the weeks following his mother's death and from that point forward never spoke of her. Magritte gave many interviews; in all of these he mentioned his mother's suicide no more than two times. Asked (rather idiotically) if the event had "marked" him, he said only that it had been a "shock." His 1954 outline for an autobiography included a single, abbreviated reference, in the third person: "In 1912, his mother, Régina, does not want to live anymore. She throws herself in Sambre."

Veils and curtains recur in Magritte's paintings, as do faces hidden behind hands or by objects, or replaced outright by a death head or an orb made of light. It's easy to guess why such images might retain so strong a hold on the artist's imagination.

The thing is, though Magritte did wake to discover that his mother's bed was empty, he never saw her body recovered from the Sambre. As a number of onlookers testified, the boy wasn't there on the riverbank.

Psychology—a science Magritte dismissed as false, an attempt to explain what cannot be explained, to render irreducible mystery to pedestrian cause and effect—calls such memories "screen memories," which typically date back to childhood. A child creates what he believes is a truth to protect himself from a truth he finds even more traumatic. But what could be worse than the scene Magritte believed he witnessed? The face of his dead mother unveiled? Her body, which he must have harbored a desire to possess, covered by a winding sheet and taken from him forever? A desire enflamed at the time of her death, when, at fourteen, he was necessarily caught up in the turmoil of adolescence and, as they still shared her bedroom, saw her in a nightdress that revealed perhaps a little more than it ought?

"It may indeed be questioned whether we have any memories at all *from* our childhood," Freud writes in his 1899 paper on the topic. "Memories *relating* to childhood may be all that we possess."

It's only when I consider my early years with an express focus on having been an only child that I understand why this story of Magritte and his mother's suicide has compelled and disturbed me for so many years. Ever since I learned of it, accidentally, while pursuing the larger topic of memory and how reliably (factually) true it might or might not be, I've revisited the scene over and over, picturing the artist as he pictured himself. I see a boy—how clearly I can imagine his form, the slope of his shoulders, the balled fists at his sides as he stands on the banks of a river to watch as the corpse of his mother is pulled from the water. Or perhaps, as my son did at that age, he holds his hands in the air when frightened, as though under arrest. Of course the body frightens the boy in its faceless nakedness, flesh I see as if rendered by the surrealist himself, white as a sheet.

Magritte and I knew only the same few facts: One night we awoke; we found our mothers' beds empty; we alerted our families; a tragedy ensued. That the artist's far more dire story included a set of ghostly footprints leading to a terrible truth would appeal, naturally, to a woman who once followed the ashy tracks of an intruder in her home, one who threatened a wish she valued above all else: that her mother had been paying close attention all along. Might the Christmas memory in question—over which I've puzzled for nearly fifty years, holding it dear, as one guards the instrument of a dangerous wound, a bullet excised, a blade pulled carefully out—never have happened? Or might it have happened very differently from the way I believe it did?

The pieces of the story are, all of them, emblematic of my early unhappiness. My mother's bed that she hadn't slept in was the bed I visited each day after she moved out, standing before the lie it spoke, its sheets changed weekly as if to suggest her return was imminent. The Christmas stocking, whose contents I fetishized and displayed each year, never playing with the toys or eating the candies but arranging them in a tableau on my dresser: What better evocation of the celebrated position of my single parent, who removed herself from the realm of the everyday mother to become a kind of holiday apparition? The night itself, when Christmas Eve becomes Christmas Day, is the one upon which a child's worthiness—naughty or nice—is judged and found either sufficient or wanting. Rehearsed as often as it was by a child filled to the brim with doctrine and consumed with the idea of her goodness and what it might afford her, if not the return of her mother then some other reward, someone else's love: I was in first grade; already I had what I needed to create an everlasting dark night of my soul.

Now I am in my fifties, and it has been decades since I learned to tell time. Now the most troubling aspect of the memory—that it was my action that caused my mother to leave—is almost too neatly textbook to be true. Don't all children hold themselves responsible for their abandonment?

Do I remember this night so vividly, with an almost hallucinatory attention to detail, because it evoked my childhood so perfectly? Or did I unconsciously collect and/or fabricate symbols of my past and assemble them into a story so I might not lose these critical aspects of myself, saved within the mnemonic device of a narrative?

Within psychotherapy, in whose arms I've spent more than twenty years, "the feelings are the facts." Which is all very well, assuming the availability of reality checks. Of, say, a brother or sister who might call me on the claim of straight A's— "There must have been a frigging B in there somewhere," he'd say. "PE," I'd answer, "and that doesn't count." But maybe it would count to my brother, the one I don't have. He might be a professional ballplayer, a perfect uncle for my young son, dreaming of his glorious future as a New York Yankee. Or what about a sister? She might say, "Piss off. You're always hiding inside your head, behind your good grades, whatever."

I didn't mind being an only child when I was a child. I understood the bargain it implied, that if I'd had siblings I would have lost my monopoly over my grandparents' affection. It might halve or even more drastically reduce my mother's infrequent attention. I knew the stresses of the family in which I'd landed: a pair of guardians who were seventy-one and sixty-two at my birth, old if not frail; a child-mother who never grew up; the endless conflicts over our dwindling financial resources. A sibling would have applied that much more pressure to what was already as frayed as the carpets and drapes, the chintz sofa. A sibling would have endangered me.

But, as an adult, having long ago reached the age at which I'd expected to have left my only childhood far behind, I mind it very much. I want a witness, or better, two, three, to recall times I recall. Not remember them as I do, but a person or persons to whom I could turn and ask, "Remember that Christmas, the one when Mom . . ."

Cat Fancy

IT IS 1972, NEARLY SIX YEARS SINCE MY MOTHER MOVED OUT OF her parents' house and into an apartment five miles away. At first she kept her address secret, but once my grandmother began paying the rent my mother was forced to reveal the location, and even invite my grandparents and me for dinner once or twice a year.

It's a tidy little apartment that came furnished, which I find curiously discouraging; I cannot yet put words to the particular sadness a laminate dining set inspires in me. But at least it's clean and neat. There's no plastic covering the couch, and there is no wallpaper hanging in strips. The drapes are not shredded to grass skirts, and during this yuletide season my mother's decorated Christmas tree is not, like ours, on its side in the middle of the living room.

Our tree is lying on the floor because the cats pull it over, once a day at least, sometimes by climbing it, but more often by pulling on the cord that delivers electricity to the colored bulbs burning among its needles. We have a lot of cats, as many as nineteen one year, but that tally included two litters of kittens. In 1967 my grandmother, whose snobbery takes various and unexpected forms (she knows, for example, the tonnage and stateroom plan of every Cunard and White Star ocean liner), discovered pedigreed Himalayans. Now, five years later, she breeds and shows them, preserving the papers that document their lineage in the same locked box with her American citizenship and her dead parents' passports. In the breeding and showing of cats, as well as other endeavors, I am my grandmother's accomplice and servant. I'm eleven, she's seventy-three; I have quick legs and sharp eyes, she's arthritic and has cataracts; I'm subservient, she's autocratic. And, to be fair, I'm devoted to her and she's sufficiently charming to convince me to do anything. Almost.

My job, this winter morning in Los Angeles, is to remove the tinsel that issues from the tiny, pink, puckered assholes of six white kittens that appear completely untroubled by their plight. Not so my grandmother, who is in hysterics.

"Help!" she cries. "Help! Help! It will cut their intestines to ribbons! Please! I beg of you!" Having chased and corralled them into the living room, where the tree lies incumbent, she collapses, breathless, on the frayed chintz sofa. Among the tattered presents, whose wrappings and ribbons have been clawed and chewed, one kitten sits swallowing more tinsel. The five others whisk among chair legs and over the coffee table, trailed by what looks disconcertingly like the silver streamers that decorated the handlebars of my first bicycle.

From a distance, the impression given by the excreted icicles is that the strands of tinsel are unaffected by their passage through the feline digestive tract. In fact, the tinsel looks the same as it did when hanging from the upright tree: silver and shiny and, well, just as tinselly as tinsel that hasn't been eaten and eliminated. But, worried that a closer inspection might render this opinion false, I refuse to heed my grandmother's stricken pleas.

"You know, Nana, I don't think I should."

"Yes! Yes! Oh, you must! Just pull it very gently, darling, that's all. Oh, I beg of you, please! Anything! I'll give you anything you like, if only you will!" But bribery won't work. There's nothing I want enough to perform this service.

"I think we should just let it . . . um, you know, just come out on its own. Otherwise it could hurt them. If I pulled."

"But it's hurting them now!" my grandmother wails, prostrate on the couch, a gnarled hand over her rheumatic heart. "It could kill them!"

"It doesn't look like it hurts. They're acting pretty much like they always do." Climbing the drapes and swinging from their slack cords, sharpening their needle-like claws on the prone tree's trunk, continuing to strip wrapping from the presents, batting loose ornaments across the rug: Only their icicle-trimmed derrieres distinguish them from the kittens they were the day before.

My grandmother struggles into an upright position to consider the litter gamboling about the rumpled white sheet used, with questionable effect, to suggest a bank of snow beneath the tree. As she includes her cats in her intense hypochondria, their complaints inspire such anxiety that I am the one who performs household veterinary functions. I preside over the confinements and labors of expectant females, administer oral medications, groom, and trim claws. I can, when necessary, give shots. With respect to medical assessments, I am my grandmother's trusted counsel, second best only to the vet himself. "Well," she says, "if you're sure they're not in pain . . ."

Released from a hideously unappetizing chore, I set to work cheerfully on a different and much preferable one: righting the tree and stripping it of whatever tinsel is left.

"I'm going to come back as one of your grandmother's cats," Libby tells me. My mother's first governess and my sometime babysitter, Libby disapproves of pets, especially those whose needs are considered before those of their human housemates. Her studio apartment on La Cienega Boulevard is very clean, and I am not allowed to sit or even lean on the twin bed, with its emerald spread.

Libby is old, nearly ninety, and frail. Her real name is Vera Libben, and she speaks often of death, and of how for the past thirty years my grandmother has "looked out" for her—bought groceries, paid bills, left money on the little folding table where she eats. I know she's joking when she speaks of her plans for reincarnation, but her voice sounds serious, as if she means it.

Practically speaking, Libby cannot babysit—she can hardly walk—and when I am left with her I wonder what I should do if she were to die.

"Do you have any relatives?" I ask her once.

"A nephew, in the old country." The old country is Russia, then the Brezhnev-era USSR, the nephew therefore of limited use. In my family of displaced Europeans, only my grandfather uses the words "Soviet Union." The rest of us serve the quaint conceit that the nineteenth-century monarchies persist. I decide that I'll call the police, if I have to.

"Off," she says, when I am drawn to her forbidden bed.

The lustrous, quilted fabric of her bedspread mystifies and tempts me for its lack of cat hair, which anoints all fabrics in our house. "Don't stand there," she says, looking at my navy wool school blazer. Even her old eyes can see that the application of yards of masking tape has not removed all the long white hairs from my school uniform. Cat hair has infiltrated our entire house; such volumes of it are washed and dried along with the laundry that when I get out of the shower and cover myself with a fresh towel, cat hair sticks to my damp skin. I learn to pat myself dry with paper towels from a roll I keep in my bathroom.

But I've embraced the cats. The old maxim "If you can't beat them, join them" applies here, and my understanding is that beating the cats is no more possible than triumphing over my grandmother herself.

My grandmother and her fellow cat fanciers have organized themselves into a club: women in and around Los Angeles who breed and show Himalayans, a hybrid of the Persian's squat body and long coat and the Siamese's markings. They spend these meetings gossiping about other breeders, some of whom euthanize substandard kittens in their freezers, an idea I find so indelibly shocking that I avoid opening the door to our own, innocent appliance, seeing the white vapor within as small ghostly animals sitting among the frozen peas and cartons of ice cream.

The cat club is exclusively female—the husbands, as far as I can tell, either dead or so self-sacrificing as to be dead. My grandfather, for example, who hates the cats, has built them what my grandmother calls their "garden house"—a concrete foundation beneath a wood frame strung with chicken wire. He outfitted the structure with wide shelves on which cats could relax while being "aired," offsetting the boredom of a life spent indoors and also aiding the growth of their thick coats, the latter a highly theoretical benefit, as the balmy Southern California weather never approaches anything that might occur in the Himalayas.

For the Santa Monica cat show, my grandmother's favorite on the show circuit—we go every year—her best cat friend, Marjorie, makes the six-hour drive to Los Angeles from where she lives, just outside of San Francisco. She drives an old wood-panel station wagon, muffler dragging, antenna bent, and stays in a nearby motel that accepts feline guests. Privately, we call her "Once for Love and Twice for Money." This is the compressed matrimonial history she delivers in lieu of more conventional introductions. Marjorie is someone for whom I have affection, a feeling perhaps inspired by her ability to make my family seem, comparatively, less peculiar.

She carries an undisclosed fortune in a little chamois pouch hung between her hanging breasts, which she clothes not in a brassiere but in one of her departed husbands' undershirts, and she shows off the pouch each time she visits. Despite her abbreviated, unsentimental description of the three gentlemen who have widowed her, Marjorie is not without emotions. In fact, she seems to harbor rather too many for my grandfather, whom she disconcertingly calls "Daddy." She praises his cooking with moist eyes whenever she comes to dinner.

"Don't mind me. You all go right ahead," Marjorie says,

waving her ringed fingers as she slowly chews her favorite dish, my grandfather's bun-less hamburgers or, as my grandmother calls them, "bullets." Marjorie looks longingly at the bottle of Heinz ketchup my grandmother has placed on the table as a test. My grandmother feels this condiment represents the worst of American culture. A saving sixth sense prevents Marjorie from reaching for it.

My grandparents, each a survivor of the Darwinian scarcity of boarding-school meals, learned long ago—my grandfather in a previous century—to eat quickly so as to secure the rare second helping. Marjorie, however, eats very slowly. She has false teeth that require periodic manipulation under her napkin and is infamous for having once removed them entirely, uppers and lowers, to rinse in a water glass at the table. I am always waiting fervently for her to repeat the performance, knowing as I do that this would require her to "take leave of her senses," my grandmother's explanation for the egregious lapse in etiquette. To be truthful, it is only my hope that I might witness madness and disgrace that sustains me through dinners with Marjorie.

For an hour or more we sit, waiting for dessert, in the fiercely uncomfortable wrought-iron chairs grouped around our glass-topped kitchen table, sighing, fidgeting, but never, alas, excusing ourselves. I don't know why we eat indoors at a table meant for outdoors, and I never think to ask. We do so many things differently from other families that patio furniture in the kitchen is of little consequence. At least the chairs encourage good posture, as whenever I slouch, a lumpen iron rose in the back of mine digs into the tender place between my shoulder blades.

Marjorie's one culinary recommendation, which she shares
with us one evening—providing anecdotal fodder for years to
come—is the economy of hanging Baggies of raw ground beef
from her California fruit trees. They frighten off birds that
might otherwise destroy her crop of cherries, and as the meat
warms in the sun, it approaches by dinnertime something akin,
she says, to steak tartare. Like the unexpected revelation of her
two sets of teeth sunk in their red plastic gums, the idea is gro-
tesque and yet it fascinates me.

My mother, who usually stops in a few times a week but
makes herself scarce during show weekends, refers to Marjorie
and my grandmother's other cat friends as "freaks." It's a fair
judgment and yet one at which I take umbrage, in that it seems
to imply that I, so thoroughly under my grandmother's sway,
am at least a latent misfit.

Why do I like cat shows? Do I like cat shows? I never ask myself the question, nor do I bother to consider if I like the cats
themselves. Neither is in any way avoidable, my preferences in
these and other areas entirely beside the point. It never occurs
to my grandmother that my friends are outside, riding bikes,
playing with their Barbies, reading in their rooms: doing what
kids from other families do. In any case, she disapproves of
other children, which I manage to take as a compliment.

Typically the shows take place in fairground halls or armor-
ies, cavernous rooms that slowly fill with cigarette smoke and
dander and the smells of used cat litter, scorching coffee, and
disinfectant. We wake at 6:00 A.M. in order to arrive by 8:00 to
register our animals and queue up before the veterinarian's
table for the required examination. As soon as we find the cages

we've been assigned, my grandmother sends me to find coffee for us both.

Cat shows are themed. They are Hawaiian, or they are Haunted Mansion, or, worst of all, Vaudevillian. My grandmother, however, does not stoop to "piffle," "twaddle," or "meaningless frivolity," so once I am revivified by the coffee, I dress her cats' cages as always, with specially tailored blue and mauve satin draperies, a fringed cover above, and a square of carpet below. If there is any irony in the pristine preservation of these satin curtains, dry-cleaned after each use, in contrast to those in the windows of our home, it is something I see only years later, with that clarity famous to hindsight. Into the blue cage goes the blue point Himalayan, whose ears, nose, paws, and tail are a frosty gray-blue color. Into the mauve cage goes the lilac point, whose analogous parts are a warmer color, not lilac, in my estimation, but what in the world of show cats makes sense? Each cat has its own miniature brass bed on which to recline and a litter box screen made of cardboard covered with flowered contact paper. The cats love these screens I made; they love them too much. Once transferred from carrier to cage, they leave their brass beds empty, preferring to crouch in the litter, hidden from the eyes of potential admirers.

As far as I can tell, cat people are divided into women who are either very fat or very thin and flagrantly homosexual men. At eleven, I do not understand what fundamentally distinguishes gay men from straight, but I recognize the men at the show as those whose interest in women is friendly rather than romantic, men who incline toward ascots, waistcoats, and other foppish attire that my grandmother ranks as "swish," "beaucoup swish," or "trop swish." The thin women, like my grandmother and Marjorie, have fat cats. Fat women, many of a girth that drives my grandmother to a fever pitch of thrilled horror, have emaciated Siamese or Cornish Rex that they drape over their massive shoulders or around their sweating necks. The sight of their huge buttocks quivering under yards of fabric excites my grandmother to flights of mathematics she can't summon for any other cause. "Ten! No, fifteen!" she cries, helpless to stop herself or even to lower her voice adequately. "I could get fifteen pairs of trousers from just one leg of hers!"

As there is no restaurant within walking distance, nor time to drive to one between judging events, we're forced to either go hungry or eat terrible food from the venue's concession: withered hot dogs turning on grease-slicked rollers; flabby, limp-bunned burgers; doughnuts with jelly bleeding through their sugared sides. "I suppose I'll just have to perish of indigestion," my grandmother says at every show. "We really ought to have brought a picnic." But we never do, for which I'm grateful, as it is my general purpose to remain as anonymous as possible, and my family's picnics involve a level of paraphernalia that raises them from meal to performance. Many of the exhibitors avoid all but the scorched coffee and chain-smoke with whichever shaking, nicotine-stained hand isn't holding a cat. At night, when we come home, our hair, clothes, and animals all reek of cigarettes. We let the cats out of their carriers and they immediately streak upstairs to hide under the beds.

I tell my grandmother eleven is too old for a babysitter, but she disagrees. She leaves me with Libby on long summer afternoons when she is at cat club meetings, and my grandfather is out visiting his family from a previous marriage. Libby takes me on the bus to the La Brea Tar Pits in Hancock Park, which I find a melancholy pilgrimage. The pits are always the same, black and oozing, with gas bubbles that rise so slowly we use Libby's wristwatch to time how long it takes one to burst.

The pits have a sinister, acrid smell, conjuring disabled automobiles and stranded travelers, and Libby always makes me read the signs aloud to her, even though she knows what they say about the animals that died there during the Ice Age, and how Indians used tar to waterproof their canoes. We've been here countless times. The family tree of ancient mammals hangs before our eyes, illustrations of mastodons and sloths and other ungainly creatures that look as though they would have been crushed by the weight of their own lumbering disappointment no matter what they stepped into. I suppose Libby, who feels she is shirking her babysitting obligations if we don't go outside, might take me to a different park; but I assume Libby doesn't know how to get to anyplace except the tar pits, and, lacking confidence in my ability to navigate Los Angeles's occult bus system, I never suggest another destination.

"Libby says she's coming back as one of your cats," I tell my grandmother, when she picks me up from what turns out to be my last visit to Libby's apartment.

"Libby doesn't like cats," my grandmother says pityingly, as if this represents further proof of Libby's impoverishment.

"But she's worried that she hasn't been wicked enough to be demoted."

"Oh, what tosh!"

———

Apparently the nephew in the old country has money, enough to have Libby installed in a nursing home. "How odd," my grandmother says upon learning of Libby's change in circumstances. "I thought no one there had money."

When we visit Libby in her little linoleum-floored room, she herself tells my grandmother that she's coming back as a cat. For a long time my grandmother doesn't answer her, but sits silently by her bed, looking out the window.

"What kind?" she finally asks.

At this I begin laughing. My grandmother wants to know why, but I can't say while we're in the room with Libby. "Because," I answer my grandmother. "Because."

In the car I explain. "It sounded as if you'd only take her if she came back as a purebred, a cat with a pedigree."

"Don't be ridiculous," my grandmother says.

"Why ask, then?"

"I was curious, that's all."

"No, you were—you were being a, a—"

"A what?"

"A snob. A cat snob."

My grandmother begins to cry, one of her tactics. "How can you? How can you say such beastly, cruel things to me? To me, who took you in?"

The fact that she did is my grandmother's trump card, and she always plays it.

"Throw me out!" I sometimes reply. "If that's how you feel about it." We both know it's a hollow threat.

Libby dies after my grandmother has stopped breeding cats. So there are no new kittens to either demonstrate or disprove Libby's promise of reincarnation. But I torment my grandmother by encouraging strays—surreptitiously leaving dry food on the patio and naming each of them "Libby." When I bring one into the house she catches it and puts it out.

I am thirty years old when my grandmother dies. I throw out all the show ribbons and trophies she kept, and I discard the remains of the cats, all the little engraved urns from Cal Pet Crematory that line her mantelpiece. Their archived pedigrees, kept in the lockbox with the passports, go in the trash. Though I know it is a betrayal, I give the last of her cats to a relative stranger—a nurse who made home visits near the end of my grandmother's life. She admired the ice-eyed animal and was thrilled to receive her.

I attempt to inoculate myself from becoming the freak my mother had seemed to predict by declaring myself a Dog Person. This is a theoretical identity, untested until our son turns seven and we get him a dog. Then it becomes a conceit.

"You just can't pick when love strikes," a veterinarian says to me, an excuse that proves useful. She's referring to the animal on the examination table between us, an unfortunate combination of beagle (loud) and terrier (determined). As I'm not looking for ways to justify owning a dog, I apply her words to our cat.

I didn't mean to. In fact I meant not to. I hadn't lived with a cat since childhood, and I thought that was behind me. But it was during a dinner party, and I'd had a glass of wine; my defenses were down. We heard an animal crying outside. My husband went to investigate.

"It's a kitten," he said.

"Ohhh," said a dinner guest, trailing off in a sigh of sympathy.

"If we take it in, that's it," I warned my husband. "We'll never get rid of it."

"Why not?" He looked puzzled.

"Because." Because I'd missed them? Because the idea of *taking her in* conjured my dead grandmother, my peculiar childhood? It was no more a happy time than she was an easy woman, and yet I missed them both. I said nothing except, "Because." So much of what we know arrives after the fact.

My husband shrugged. Who could sit down to a dinner of scampi while a starveling begged piteously at the door? He retrieved the kitten, a scrap of a tabby weighing less than a pound. The sympathetic guest donated one of her prawns, holding it out to the animal.

"No, wait." I took it from her to wash off the garlic, minced it into a saucer's worth of morsels. Though I intended to remain aloof, unaffected, I couldn't take my eyes off the kitten. I wanted the guests to go home and leave me to what appeared, suddenly and unexpectedly, a greater pleasure than their company. I watched as the kitten washed herself after eating—face, whiskers, paws—grooming all she could reach, and felt a kind of . . . what? Well-being, I suppose. If not security, then something close to that. Under what circumstances, however dire, would a cat forgo the rituals of washing?

We carried dessert to the living room and the kitten followed, purring. Another thing I'd forgotten: the seduction of that noise reserved for happiness, contentment. I put down my coffee cup to examine her, looking in her ears and eyes, opening her mouth with my finger, running my hand along her spine. "Mites," I said of her infested ears, feeling the purr vibrate to the end of her tail. "I'll have to get some ear drops."

"Did you have some kind of veterinary training?" one of our guests asked.

"No. Why?"

"Just the way you're handling it," she said. "Practiced."

"Yes," I said. "We—I—my grandmother and I—we had a lot of cats when I was a child."

I set the kitten on the floor and she considered me, eye to eye. I'd tried to like the dog, but who would have thought she'd be so predictably doggy? So ingratiating, so slavish in devotion? Considering the kitten, not two months old and already fully enigmatic, self-contained, discriminating in displays of affection, I found myself wondering if the dog didn't remind me of my child self: too eager to please. The dog had come from a shelter. Did this explain why she seemed, each and every day, so grateful to have been taken in?

The kitten didn't consider herself the recipient of charity. In the midst of the dinner party she walked slowly among guests and furnishings, not so much taken in as deciding whether or not to stay. At this writing, she's eleven years old, asleep on the red velvet tuffet in my study. When she walked in, my feet were propped on it. She sat, silent, waiting, until I moved them.

Baby New Year

"I'm lost," my grandmother tells me. She's calling me at work, where, in New York, it's about four in the afternoon. She's in Los Angeles, three hours behind and three thousand miles away.

"What do you mean, 'lost'?"

"I mean I haven't the faintest idea where I am!" Behind her indignant voice I can hear traffic, freeway traffic, a sound familiar to anyone who's ever lived in L.A.—a noise of rushing air, of atmosphere displaced by velocity. It's a sound so familiar that I never noticed it until long after I'd moved away and returned as a visitor.

"Where were you going?" I ask my grandmother.

"To the dentist."

"In Pasadena?"

"Yes. Yes. You know, Dr. Bendel."

"So you're calling from a pay phone?"

"What do you think!"

"You don't have to snap at me. You were going northbound on 101?"

"Yes."

"Then what?"

"I don't know. I don't know. I missed the turn or—I don't know! All of a sudden I didn't recognize any of the exits." There is panic in her voice. Just the previous weekend I had yet another argument with my soon-to-be husband, who demanded why I still hadn't written—why I refused to write—to the Department of Motor Vehicles to ask that my grandmother's driver's license be revoked. Was it because I didn't care if she ran over someone?

"It isn't only herself she's jeopardizing," he said.

"You just don't get it. You don't know L.A. There's no public transportation, not like here in New York, not within walking distance. And she's alone. Without a car she can't even get to the market."

"She can take cabs."

I didn't answer. Of course she shouldn't be driving, not at ninety, balanced on a thick cushion on top of a phone book to achieve enough altitude to see over the steering wheel of her outsize Lincoln. She's nervous and "a bit hard-of-hearing" and she sees other drivers through the smeary haze of eyeglasses whose lenses she never remembers to clean, lenses she literally butters at breakfast, putting down her toast to push her glasses up from where they've slid down her nose. She's so deaf that even with her hearing aids turned up she can't understand me if I don't raise my voice. Certain of my co-workers have become an enthusiastic audience for her calls, which I receive regularly. She has four aged cats, two with pancreatitis, the symptoms of which she reports in gruesome detail, along with her valiant and creative failures to disguise their little enzyme pills in lumps of liverwurst or folded squares of lox. A third has an inoperable brain tumor and is taken with "fits." The Mexican cleaning lady kindly brings her homemade tamales, which give her indigestion, which in turn inspires her calling me to suggest the indigestion is actually cardiac arrest. Her legs tingle, presaging cerebral hemorrhage. She has a "poisoned" toe. What does it mean, do I think, if she sees falling "twinkles" in her left eye? There are prowlers in the back, and vandals in the front. All these reports interrupt and disturb me, sometimes to the point of tears. I'm the only family she has left, after all. But it's the roadside emergencies that eventually dismantle the defensive stance I maintain with regard to my grandmother. My husband keeps warning me that the responsibility for the deaths of her innocent victims will be mine.

"What exit did you take?" I ask her, watching the LED readout just over my phone's keypad, the one that counts off the seconds, minutes, even—potentially—the hours, of a conversation.

"I don't know."

"Well, can you tell me what street you're on now?"

"I'm at an Exxon station."

"Did you ask the attendant for directions?"

"He's a lout."

"I don't care if he's a lout. Did you ask him for help?"

"A foreign lout! I couldn't understand a word he said!"

"Okay," I say, "okay." The one critical thing to remember about a call like this is not to make her cry. When she does, she gets even more rattled and confused, and uses this against me. Reflexively—it's not strategy but habit—she'll amplify and prolong the noise of her crying to make me feel like a monster, to remind me that if she's alone and helpless, it's my fault. I'm the one who's left her. (Or, to be accurate, among those who've left her I am the only living and therefore, practically speaking, accountable person.) "Did you try calling Triple A?" I ask.

"They don't come unless the car breaks down."

"You called them?"

She says nothing.

"What's the point of being a member? You do pay annual dues, you know."

Silence, except for the ambient noise of cars rushing past. I am the de facto guardian of an irrational and contrary nonagenarian. I wonder if, from my desk in New York, I could call the Automobile Club of Southern California and convince a dispatcher to send someone in a tow truck to find my grandmother and drag her home. A long shot, at best. And I'd have to put my grandmother on hold, presenting the risk that she'll hang up and throw herself on the mercy of the first likely young woman she sees, one whom, if she snags her, she will try to fashion into a surrogate for me. My grandmother will take this Samaritan to lunch or dinner, buy her a snowboard or contact lenses or a new carburetor—whatever she wants, whatever my grandmother believes will cement the girl's nascent fealty to her. My grandmother will call to tell me about the many sterling qualities this young woman possesses. At last, usually after a "misunderstanding"—this is the word my grandmother used to describe the disappearance of a small color television from her home—the girl will betray my grandmother: She'll disappear, change her phone number, stand her up for lunch. So, forget the automobile club.

"Okay, Nana," I say. "This isn't a crisis. Tell me what street you're on. Read me the sign. And the cross street, too."

It takes time to guide my grandmother back to her house, nearly an hour when I add in two more calls from pay phones en route. But I do get her there. I've driven her to the dentist so many times that I know the tangle of freeway interchanges between her house and his office well enough to guess which wrong turn she took. Having grown up in Los Angeles, driving since I was fifteen, I can navigate its streets, even from a distance. But I can't stop my grandmother from losing her way, or from talking to strangers. Or, and especially, from hitting another car.

My husband and I have been married three months, barely, when he makes an announcement. My grandmother, he says, is about to develop from a problem into a crisis. He sees it coming. What's more, he knows that the best way of averting inevitable disaster is to move her east, to live near—with—us.

"You can't be serious," I say. He has made this outrageous announcement in the course of one of our unhurried, postprandial walks through our neighborhood, block after block of graceful old homes. Brownstones, mostly, some with bay windows before which we pause to picture ourselves on the other side of the glass. I pull up short. He stops, too, and looks at me.

"Why not?" he says.

"Why not!"

"Yes. Why not?"

"You have no idea what you're saying. You've never lived with her. You don't know what she's like."

He waves a hand through the air, as if dismissing a gnat. "She's an old woman."

"What is that supposed to mean?"

"How hard could it be? I mean, really?"

"Oh my God! Why do you think my mother fled? What do you think I'm doing on the opposite coast?"

Just because my grandmother is ninety years old, less than five feet tall, and eighty-something pounds, is not reason to underestimate her power to drive a person crazy. Demanding, conflicted, inconsistent (but not consistently so), selfish as well as given to gestures of extravagant (often self-interested) generosity, insecure, witty but not wise, suggestible, manipulative, histrionic, and, yes, very charming and funny: She's the life of the party, as long as it's her party.

"It's like this," I try to explain. "You can't even sit on a couch with her. No matter what she's doing, no matter how apparently quiet and still she's being, you can't be in the same room with her and manage to read a book. Or even one page of a book. Or think a single coherent thought. You haven't spent enough time with her to find this out, but she's a human vacuum, a black hole. She just wants wants wants and you can't ever give her enough. She pulls you in and consumes you. Even when she isn't making a sound she's loud. Deafening."

"Don't you think you're being a little dramatic?"

"Not really. She's not a grandmother the way people think of grandmothers. She's not the Waltons. She's more Auntie Mame meets the Addams family." I imagine her standing in her kitchen, laboriously cutting up raw beef heart to feed to her cats. It takes so long that she's always interrupted at the task, and she forgets to wash her hands before answering the phone or responding to the buzzer on the clothes dryer. The trim around the doors, painted white, the wall where the phone hangs, also white, the doorknobs and cupboards and the cutlery drawer—the laundry itself, freshly washed and dried—

everything is anointed with bits of raw flesh that dry and stick with a fierceness rivaling that of epoxy. To pick even one surface clean requires dedication—were the housekeeper to attempt removing all the meat, she'd have time for nothing else—and so the house always looks as if it's recently hosted a murder, a messy killing at the hands of a psychopath unconcerned with being found out.

As I never invited friends home to see the meat on the walls, or hear my grandmother's screams of rage when anyone crossed her, no one ever understood what I meant when I said she was "difficult." If a friend or colleague met her, it was at a restaurant or a party, where she told antic, exotic, and often very funny or dramatic tales of growing up in China, or taking a refugee Russian prince as a lover in Nice, and other stories involving her eccentric family, of whom a disproportionate number were sexually deviant and/or inclined to wave pistols and threaten suicide over minor romantic mishaps. There was, too, the escape from Nazis, complete with slavering "Alsatians," which always sounded more foreign and thrilling than "German shepherds." Undeniably, she was charming, right down to her poisoned toe.

"Look," my husband says. "If she doesn't run over someone, she's going to fall down the stairs and break her hip. Or go off the deep end and leave all her money to her cats."

"Fine. Let her."

"When she breaks her hip or wrecks the car and gets taken to court, or when her heart finally gives out, it's going to be a lot worse to deal with from a distance. Think of what it was like when your mother was dying, or your grandfather. Weren't things difficult enough when you were there, in the same city?"

We keep walking, both of us silent. It's January, dark and

cold. The gray ice underfoot is indistinguishable from the stone sidewalk, to the eye, anyway. It's slippery, and the cold comes through the leather soles of my shoes and makes my feet ache. I know what's coming next; it's only a matter of time—two blocks, as it turns out—before my husband reminds me of our last visit to my grandmother's house, when he found shingles blowing off the roof and an open box of blank personal checks left on the back porch, its contents scattered over the ill-tended property.

"Here's another way to look at it," he says as we turn the corner onto our own block. "If we were to help your grandmother put her house on the market, sell it, and move her east to live with us, then we could pool our resources. Together, the three of us would be able to put enough money down on a house to carry the balance for about as much as we're spending on rent. Real estate is insane in Los Angeles, and it's going to crash. She'll never get more for that house than she would now."

The lit window of someone's dining room makes a silhouette of his head as he talks. I try to imagine my grandmother navigating the ice under my feet. She hasn't worn shoes with closed toes for decades. For formal occasions she has a pair of black suede sling-backs that invite her big toes to poke through in front. For everything else it's the flat beige sandals, their straps worn loose to accommodate her bunions—so loose that a few years earlier, one of them caught on the accelerator pedal while she was flying down Ventura Boulevard. Unable to brake as she approached an intersection, she came to a stop against a telephone pole, after crushing three fiberglass dune buggies parked in front of a car dealership.

"Aren't you forgetting something?" I say as my husband unlocks the door to our apartment.

"What?"

"She doesn't want to live with us."

"Not even if she had a separate floor? Most of these houses are carved up into two or more units, anyway."

"She hates New York."

"She hasn't been here in, what, thirty years? Forty?"

"Okay, she thinks she hates New York. It's the same difference."

"She could bring her cats."

"Even so."

Despite my apprehension about living with my grandmother and her insistence that she'd rather die alone, in agony, than move to the East Coast, my standard response to her panic calls is to remind her that none of it—the dead car battery, the prostrate pet, the overflowing toilet, the clogged rain gutters, the carrot peeler stuck in the garbage disposal—would present much of a problem were she living under the same roof with me and my husband. But comfort and safety are not, finally, the enticement she requires. We both know this; she does and so do I. There is an offer she can't refuse, but I haven't made it, not yet.

"I don't know a single soul in New York!" she says. "Not a soul!"

"Nana. You don't know anyone in L.A. anymore, either."

"There's Eula."

"She's in Oxnard. Sixty miles away."

"Crystal."

"You just told me she has terminal stomach cancer."

"And Rosa. What about Rosa?"

"The housekeeper doesn't count. And neither does the doctor or the dentist. Or the gardener, who, by the way, is ripping you off. He's stolen every tool out of Poppa's shed."

"So why don't you move back, if you're so worried about me?"

"Because I'm twenty-eight. I have a job. Here. In New York. We both do. You're ninety. You're the one with the house you can't take care of, and the sick cats you can't get to the vet, and the car you can't drive without getting lost. Why can't you be flexible for once in your life?"

My grandmother slams the phone down. I look up and see the marketing director leaning in the doorway. "Nana?" she asks. By now everyone in my department is bored by our phone calls, but my grandmother's just catching on in other divisions.

I don't have to ask the DMV to take her license away. It expires, and she fails the written test required for its renewal. Given the opportunity to prove herself on an actual road test, with an examiner in the passenger seat, she gets so nervous that she drives over the little concrete wall around the flower bed behind the DMV offices, right through the plants and over the ornamental tree in the middle. When she bumps down off the other side of the bed, the examiner tells her she can park her car now—the test is over. They both get out and consider the shrubs hanging from the front bumper. "I'm afraid I have to fail you, ma'am," he tells her.

"This is your fault," she tells me.

The last two times her license was about to expire, I flew to
Los Angeles and accompanied her to the DMV, where we ren-
dezvoused in the women's room so she could pass me her un-
completed test under the metal wall dividing two stalls. Twice,
I made myself a criminal for my grandmother. I sat on a public
toilet and took the official Department of Motor Vehicles written driver's test in her stead—a federal offense, for all I knew—
then passed it back, including a token mistake or two. The first
time I did this, she tricked me into it, causing a scene at the
DMV by turning her handbag upside down in the examination
area and surreptitiously shoving the test in my hands when I
came forward to catch the rolling red lipstick and smelling
salts. The second time, I didn't bother to resist. Instead, I pil-
fered one of her tranquilizers to get myself through the ordeal
without my hands shaking. The government employee who
graded the test scrawled a big red *P* for "pass" on top, and directed my grandmother to the camera that recorded her trium-
phantly smiling picture. A month later, she got her renewed
license in the mail: Crime did pay.

"You know it's your fault!" she wails into the phone. "I'm
no good at tests. I get nerve-racked. I want you to write a letter
to the DMV and tell them so."

"Come on, Nana. I can't do that."

"Why not!"

"Because part of being a safe driver is not getting nerve-
racked. Last time around, I knew you could drive without—"

"Oh, what tosh! I've been driving since I was fourteen. I
was all over the Italian Alps in my Hispano-Suiza before that,
that . . . officious lout's father was in short pants!"

To allow my grandmother to be frail, to depend on me in her old age as I, during childhood, depended on her: In this I'm forced to recognize the loss of her license for what it is, a harbinger of her death. Despite her careless cruelties, despite her having psychologically dismantled my young mother and then, after taking me on, presided over a household so bizarre that she blighted whatever chance I might have had at being a socially tolerated teenager, she is my family, my only remaining family. I love her, and I find her as charming as she is impossible. I see the bravado required to be funny and beguiling when what you really are is old and aching and breathless from congestive heart failure, when what you really are is afraid. And I know—I haven't forgotten—that many times, every day of my early life, it was she who stood between me and the world, she who was the parent my mother couldn't be. If she failed us, it was in the force of her desire, her need. She wanted my mother and me, wanted us absolutely and irrevocably, for herself, forever, and she didn't protect us from that hunger.

She's still ravenous, insatiable. And it's life she wants to consume—new life. There isn't a pram or stroller she doesn't chase for a chance to ogle the baby within, not one young mother she doesn't pump for details of her offspring's birth, its sleeping habits and digestion, the new tooth breaking through its wet smile. Every summer of my childhood we visited the San Diego Zoo; it was a pilgrimage. While my grandfather and I went off together, riding the tram from one exhibit to the next, my grandmother stood alone at the big viewing window of the primate nursery. Rapt, she watched the keepers diaper and feed infant chimpanzees, orangutans with their halos of orange fuzz, and, once, a little lowland gorilla with its strangely exhausted face, black bags under its eyes. She gasped audibly with delight when one of the blue-uniformed young women put down a bottle of formula to lift an ape over her shoulder and burp it. "Do you want one?" I'd ask my grandmother, feeling almost jealous. She'd hug herself, ecstatic.

"Bless their little furry hearts!" she'd say.

"I know how to convince her," I tell my husband. It's a weekend morning. He looks up from the paper and raises his eyebrows.

"I'll tell her that if she comes east, we'll have a baby. I'll stop using birth control as soon as she moves. Otherwise, who knows how long it might be before we could afford a bigger place? She might not live to see a great-grandchild."

My husband looks at me, nodding slowly, frowning. "Do you think that will work?"

"I know it will."

My husband stares at the wall, the newspaper, still intact, in his lap. "Would we, do you think? Would we have a baby, just like that?"

"I don't know. I mean, how would I know?"

We've never discussed having children, not really. I think we assume they'll happen as marriage did: without deliberation. It's not that either of us is careless or casual, but only three days after our first date my not-yet husband, whom I'd recently met in graduate school and with whom I'd spent an aggregate of six or seven hours, handed me the key to his front door. And, without hesitating, I took it; I moved in with him. Over the years we've discovered that with us it's always like this. No matter how large the transition, our approach to it feels as if it has been choreographed, steps we learned so long ago we can't remember when we didn't know them. Neither of us proposed to the other. We married about a year after we told his parents.

"You'd go off birth control?"

"Yes."

"And if you went off birth control . . ." He stops speaking, his eyes not focused on anything in the room.

"Eighteen months."

"Eighteen months?"

"They say that's the average. The average time it takes. Or the time it takes the average couple."

"To have a baby?"

"To conceive a baby."

"Huh," he says. He pulls out the Metro section.

"Well?"

"No."

"No?"

"No."

"Come on, Nana."

"I've lived in Southern California for more than fifty years. Of all the places in the world I might have settled, I chose here."

"I know. But—"

"Fifty!"

She flogs us through the familiar story of her visit, at seventeen, to Pasadena, where her father had taken her—by ship, from China—for a change of scene, i.e., separation from a problematic suitor. He bought her a chestnut quarter horse, had it outfitted with a Western-style saddle that was trimmed with Mexican silver, and watched her tear through the orange groves on the animal's back. Somehow, he finagled an invitation for her to ride in the Rose Parade on New Year's Day, 1916, the pretty mare's mane braided with ribbons, her neck wreathed in flowers. Even in the context of an argument, it's a story I love, and not only for my grandmother's evocation of a primeval, unspoiled California. Her affection, still so palpable, for her father—a poor boy from Baghdad who, by his wits and determination, made himself into a fabulously wealthy banker—changes her voice, softens it. When talking about her father, she sounds, I realize as I listen, less hungry.

My grandmother doesn't concede immediately, despite the offer of a great-grandchild. How can she admit she's arrived in a place she never planned to visit, the one between a rock and a hard place? In truth, neither of us wants to face the symmetry of our relationship: Just as it was she who protected my infancy, who bathed and fed and diapered me, it is I who will guard her through senescence and be midwife to her death.

I am all she has, and this frightens both of us. So we argue geography.

"Fine. You like California—"

"Love."

"You love California. But it's not as if you go to the beach. Or do business with movie producers. You don't grow strawberries or manage a motel in Santa Monica. And you don't drive."

Her voice acquires a stronger, almost plummy, British accent. "I suppose it's foolish of me to imagine that you might understand what climate means to someone who was raised in Shanghai."

"You never even go outside!"

"I look out the window."

"There are windows in New York."

"Yes, but not any I want to look out of."

"How do you know?"

She coughs in lieu of answering.

"Anyway," I say, "all this is beside the point. The bottom line is, if you come live with us, I'll have a baby."

"And you won't otherwise? For you, having a baby depends on where I choose to live?"

"Yes."

"Don't be absurd."

"As far as you're concerned, it does. Because no matter when I have a baby, if you're in L.A., you'll hardly ever see her. Or him."

Silence.

"Well?"

"I'm not discussing it any further. Not today."

"Fine. We don't have to discuss it. Are you going to move?"

"No."

"Nana."

"No."

"Are you?"

"I'll think about it."

"I knew you'd say yes!"

"I didn't say yes. I detest New York, and I didn't say yes."

The thing to do now is nothing. After a day or two of silence from my end, she'll call to say her cats' claws need cutting, or the oven doesn't work anymore, or she's lost the tax documents she needs. Under one or another pretext, she'll wait for me to bring up the idea of the move, which I won't, and my not mentioning it will make her nervous. Perhaps I've reconsidered; perhaps I don't want to take her on, after all. Mean, but efficient. I know what I'm doing.

But when she calls, it's without an excuse, and after a few minutes of small talk—in her prime, she'd have lasted far longer—she says, "I've given it some thought."

"Given what some thought?"

"Your suggestion."

"Oh?"

"I've decided to do it."

I don't gloat. "Really?" I say. "That's great!"

"Yes."

We're very cool, very casual. Pretending, perhaps, that it's just a visit, an extended visit.

Which, as it turns out, it is. In less than two years, my grandmother's rheumatic heart, its valves damaged by a childhood bout of scarlet fever, will at last give out, so enlarged at the very end that from across the room it will be possible to see it beating beneath her ribs. Still, she will have lived to become a great-grandmother. I keep my end of the bargain and get pregnant almost immediately.

"I thought you told me eighteen months," my husband says.

"On average. I must be the woman who balances out someone on the other end of the curve, one of the women who take three years."

"I guess so." He nods, slowly.

"I know it's fast," I say into his shirt, hugging him.

"All the more reason to get a babysitter sooner rather than later," he says.

We wait until it's obvious, even to me, the one who doesn't want to see it, that my grandmother can't be left alone in the house. In the ground-floor apartment of the brownstone she helps us to buy, she has a soft, new couch (a loveseat, but it looks like a couch when she sits on it) and a big television that she won't stay put in front of while we're at work. Instead, she roots compulsively through boxes of old papers, rereading and tearing up letters— "saving you the trouble," she says to me tartly—and going back and forth to her tiny kitchen to make tea, forgetting the tea, and burning the bottoms out of five different kettles. She trips over the corners of rugs or the tails of her cats, all four of which fly east with her. She spills kitty litter on the hardwood floor, inviting a fall.

She calls me at work several times a day to announce what it is she's dropped or broken, or where she's fallen, or that she can't get the faucet to turn on, or off, or that she's lost a cat, or broken a tooth: The list is long, then longer. I, in turn, call my husband, who (to spare me, in my morning sickness, another subway commute) forfeits his lunch hour to go home and sweep up litter or throw out the most recently burned kettle or, once, lift my grandmother herself off the floor. After falling down mid-conversation, she dropped the receiver where it picked up the sounds of her cursing me, as she crawled from one corner of the little apartment to another, looking for something with which to right herself. "Left me. Left me all alone," she spat to the empty room, her voice just as mean—meaner—as it was when I was a teenager fifteen years before. "Dreadful girl. Chit of a girl. How could she. Leave me. To marry that lout."

It's predictable, so why don't I predict it? When the baby comes, a little girl, my grandmother isn't happy. She's jealous. For by now she is the baby, my baby, the one whom we moved to New York so I could make her breakfast and dinner and bathe her each morning. And diaper her—that, too, toward the end. Not that she admits to envy. When she was little, she had a baby brother and wished him ill, and after that, he died. In her heart, if not her head, she believes that jealousy of babies is wicked. To banish it, she criticizes me. With respect to my little girl, I do everything wrong. I give her the wrong name. I spoil her by picking her up when she cries. I tease her by encouraging her to reach for a toy. I use the wrong baby soap: That's why she has a rash on her cheek. Worst of all, I nurse my baby. Rather than feed her formula from a bottle, I give her myself, my body. I allow (encourage!) this interloper to eat me up.

"It's plebeian," my grandmother says of breastfeeding. It's what animals do. Aboriginals. Destitute mothers who can't buy formula. "We saw them in the street in Shanghai, you know. Women with their breasts pulled out until they looked like razor strops. Their filthy children ran alongside them without letting go." She shudders fastidiously. "No woman who cared about her décolleté would ever consider it." She gives me a sharp and knowing look, easy to translate: Go on nursing that baby and your husband will no longer find you attractive. Nurse your children and he'll leave you for a woman with breasts that haven't been "mauled."

But I don't stop. Nursing is one of the few things I can do while sitting with my grandmother on the couch, both she and the baby inclined to doze, leaving me free, at least psychically. With the baby in my arms, I listen to my grandmother breathe as she sleeps, air whistling faintly as it moves through her chest. One of her hands rests on the couch between us, and I take it in mine, surprised as always by the heat of it, as if she has a fever. On her forearm are two new scars, pink and square. My fault—trying to spare her pain, I pulled off a Band-Aid too quickly, and her skin, so thin it's almost transparent, came off with the adhesive. She didn't cry, not even at all the blood, but I did.

New Year's Eve. We throw a party. The baby, representing 1991, the year written on an index card pinned to her pajamas, sleeps through the clamor of midnight, her head lolling on my shoulder. My grandmother, wearing 1990, takes my hand to help her up from the couch, and when she turns around I see the skirt of her new white wool dress is crimson, heavy with blood. On this, the first day of 1991, the year only one minute old, my grandmother will be in the hospital for tests to determine where it's all coming from, all the blood leaking from her. The old year is indeed dying, the symmetry, the one we didn't want to see, unavoidable now.

She comes home; she sleeps in a hospital bed; nurses visit, but not often enough or for long enough. Having shaved away hours once reserved for sleep to care for my grandmother as well as my daughter without having to quit my job, I am always tired, and easily brought to tears. I get up at 5:45 to nurse my ten-month-old daughter until 6:30, when I take her downstairs with me to rouse my grandmother, always hesitating at the door to her apartment, praying, *Don't let her be dead,* or, sometimes, *Please let her be dead.* I find her awake in her bed, waiting to be taken to the bathroom, to be stripped and bathed and dried and diapered, then dressed in a fresh housecoat and led to the couch, where she waits for her breakfast. As it is my husband who goes to my grandmother during the night—we've set up a baby monitor in her room so as not to miss her cries—I try not to wake him before eight, when he has to get up for work, and so the baby crawls around the apartment un-supervised while I tend to my grandmother in the bath. This is okay, I think: There are no stairs to fall down, the electric outlets are baby-proofed, the cabinet under the kitchen sink emptied of cleansers. One morning, however, when I emerge from the bathroom with my grandmother, I find my little girl sitting next to the cats' bowl, her pink cheeks crammed with Friskies.

"You see?" my grandmother says, delighted. "You see how hungry she is? It's rubbish, this idée fixe you have about formula being unnatural!" The baby cries when I try to empty her mouth of the cat food, pleasing her great-grandmother. She grabs at my wrist with her little hands and turns her face away.

I must have known all along that it would come to this. That I would have to choose between them. My husband's parents arrive for a visit and cannot hide their shock at the state of the house and its occupants. We can't continue as we have been, they tell us gently. The worry on their faces shows us what a mirror can't. All new fathers are tired, but not so tired that when they get down on the floor to play with their babies they fall asleep. And a lot of women lose weight while breastfeed-ing, but not like this. We've engaged a practical nurse to help care for my grandmother in the mornings, and a full-time babysitter does whatever tidying she can during those minutes not taken by the baby, but the end of each workday still con-fronts us with dinner, laundry, dishes, and two people with overwhelming needs. Weekends are worse; it seems impossible that two days can last so long. Or that, living in the same house and sleeping in the same bed, my husband and I, so recently married, see so little of each other.

"I can't," I say to my mother- and father-in-law. "How can I, when I promised her? I promised, no matter what, I'd never put her in a home."

"But is this what she'd want for the baby?"

No. Not her old self, anyway. The grandmother who took care of me as a child would think it wrong for her great-granddaughter to be passed back and forth between parents too tired to smile. But the woman she's become might not agree. To whom do I owe the best of myself? My grandmother, who remade her life for me? Or my child, who has been in the world for little more than a year? Thirteen months, that's all, since my heart was hung above her head, filling the dark with its sound.

The social worker describes it as a "convalescent hospital," and supplies me with the lie that makes it possible for me to betray her—for her to accept what she knows is my necessary be-trayal. After being hospitalized for an ailment that fails to end her life, my grandmother is transferred to the Greenpark Care Center, where she goes to "convalesce."

The first few times I visit, I come alone. Then, one Saturday, I bring my daughter. Eighteen months old, no longer a baby, she runs past wheelchairs in the corridors, past their skeletal inhabitants, some of whom reach toward the fleeting glimpse of plump new life. When we enter my grandmother's room, she stops short of the bed, and the two of them regard each other solemnly.

"Growing," my grandmother observes, and she asks where I bought the dress my little girl is wearing. Then she changes the subject. She is less inquisitive about her only great-grandchild than I remember her being about anonymous babies in strangers' buggies. I wait a few weeks before trying again, but once more my daughter's presence makes the two of us awkward with each other, and I don't bring her back.

Along with maintaining the lie that it's only a matter of time before my grandmother comes home, together the two of us pretend that home doesn't include my daughter. It's not that we say she doesn't exist; we just don't mention her. Instead, our conversations take us back, past my childhood and my mother's, to my grandmother's own beginnings, a world and a lifetime apart.

"Isn't it remarkable," she says, "how much I remember?" The names of all the teachers at the little day school in Shanghai's International Settlement, the name of the seamstress who came to the house to measure her for dresses. Her pet rabbits, their names, and the names of all their offspring. The brand of talcum powder preferred by her governess, and the day of her birth. The Presbyterian missionary who lived down the street, his wife, their four daughters, and all their names and birthdays. In fact, she is remarkable with birthdays; she remembers every one she ever knew.

———

Except mine. On the day I turn thirty, the month and day writ very large on the wall calendar opposite her bed, my grand-mother takes my hand and pulls me close and asks me did I forget to buy a card for a distant cousin whose birthday falls three days later. "No," I tell her. "I did get one. Don't you re-member? You signed it." To hide my face from her, I step into the hall.

It doesn't matter, I tell myself. Don't let such a little thing matter. It's a part of the bargain we struck, that's all.

The thought arrives with the weight of truth. I dry my eyes. How has my grandmother's failure to acknowledge my birthday been transformed from injury into something more like a minor side effect, painful, perhaps, but without impor-tance? I am trying to understand. Somewhere in the calculus of births and deaths, in the trading of homes and the reversal of roles, in the loss of her daughter and the arrival of mine, that date, the one when my mother gave her what she never ex-pected, the second child she wanted but couldn't conceive, was lost.

"Listen," she said when I was twelve, and she seventy-four. She'd backed me into the linen closet. "If you get into trouble, I don't want you to have an abortion. Give me the baby."

I said nothing.

"Do you understand?"

I nodded.

"Promise?"

"Yes," I said, "I promise."

The Unseen Wind

*Nature gives you the face you have at twenty, life shapes
the face you have at thirty, but at fifty you get the face
you deserve.*

—Coco Chanel

I'M TWENTY WHEN MY FATHER LOOKS AT ME AND SAYS, "YOU
know, you've never seen your real self. I have, but all you've
seen is your reflection in the mirror. An image that looks very
much like you but isn't the same as you. Not really, not exactly."

"Why wouldn't it be exactly the same?" I ask, irritated because he's always doing this: telling me why I belong to him
and not to myself.

He explains that light is lost inside a mirror; a reflected

image lacks the luminous property of the object itself. As an experienced photographer, he conveys authority about such things. "Try it," he says, and he pulls me next to him before a mirror. "Look at me," he says. "Look at the real me here beside you, and then look at my reflection. They aren't the same. You'll see they aren't the same."

I don't want my father to be right. I don't want him to own what he says he does, the way I really look, leaving me with an approximation of myself, inexact and indistinct, no better than a second-generation photocopy. But when I compare the actual man to his image, I see he's right, they aren't the same. The mirror father is dimmer, duller, not quite alive.

So it's true, what he says: I have never and will never see the real me.

The divine ratio of phi—1:1.618—determines what nature gives us. Phi unwinds the chambers of a nautilus and the spiral of a galaxy, arranges seeds in the head of a sunflower. Phi is the principle on which Leonardo da Vinci based his illustration of a perfectly proportioned human being, arms and legs spread wide, the top of his head, the tips of his fingers, and the soles of his feet all points on a single circle. 1:1.618 is the length of the hand compared to that of the forearm, the width of the face to its length, the width of an eye to that of the mouth, of the eye's iris to the eye itself. Phi is the mathematical constant, sometimes called the "golden mean," exemplified in Renaissance portraits and in the portfolios of Ford models.

Symmetry. Harmony. Balance. These are beauty's terms, her demands. Exacting, like Coco Chanel. I don't fulfill them. I know this before I do the math, dividing the length of my face by its breadth, comparing the width of my mouth to that of my eye. It's too long, my face, either that or too narrow. My ears are where they ought to be, but they're too small. And while no one's features are absolutely symmetrical, I think mine may be a little more off-kilter than most. Or perhaps it's this I notice first when looking in a mirror: a lack of symmetry.

I cover one side of my face to analyze the other. The woman on the left is approachable, engaged, pensive, but not so preoccupied that a stranger would hesitate to ask directions, say, or inquire if she's using the empty chair at her table. The right-hand woman is another story, an altogether darker character. Not sinister, but hidden deep within herself. Aloof. She must be the one I hear described as icy.

"'The ice queen'—that's what we called you, when you came in for your first interview," a co-worker tells me when I'm twenty-seven.

"You're kidding," I say.

"No, really. That's how you came across before we got to know you." We laugh because, as it's turned out, I'm often the first to poke fun at myself or crack a joke in a meeting, to let down my guard in hopes others will, too. I know what my co-worker means, though. No one has ever put it to me quite so starkly, but the shock I feel when he says the words *ice queen* is one of recognition.

"You have to smile at people," my husband tells me. We haven't been married long, not even a year. "You have to look people in the eye and smile at them when you meet them," he says. "Otherwise they think you're unfriendly. I know you're uncomfortable with people you've just met, I know how shy you are, but they don't. They don't know you like I do."

Slowly—it takes ten years or more—I teach myself to be

the left side of my face when in company, congenial company, anyway.

The right side does have her place; she can be useful. The right guards her thoughts, whatever they may be, discouraging idle conversation and unwanted confidences. She isn't rude or unkind; she'd give up the unused seat at her table. But a stranger might be wary of asking her for it. Seated next to her on a train or an airplane, other passengers don't try to draw her into a dialogue. Without speaking, she makes it clear she doesn't want to talk; she protects me—my privacy, my space, and my time. It's she who ensures I can read my book uninterrupted.

My eyes account for the difference. The left opens wider; its brow is half a centimeter higher than the right's, enough that it alone is visible above the frames of most glasses. Because the left eye is wider, literally more open to inspection, it appears to welcome the curiosity of strangers, while the right remains comparatively hooded, defended if not defensive.

I smile at myself in the mirror, trying to discern if the woman I see is a friendly-looking person. Does the mood that divides my face account for the fact that the left corner of my mouth is curled, very slightly, upward into a smile, while the right corner is neutral and betrays nothing? I frown, as I do when I'm concentrating, to make sure the frown doesn't look ill tempered. But what use is this? Any face I make for myself is self-conscious, artificial; it tells me nothing about how I might appear to others. My real self, the person the rest of the world sees, is someone I barely catch a glimpse of. But there is one trick I attempt to master. In my thirties, entranced by a friend's ability to raise one eyebrow independently of the

other—entranced by her in general, as she is very charming—
I determine to teach myself how to do it, how to make a silent
inquiry or convey disapproval more subtly than words allow.
But I can't get the hang of it. It never appears effortless or natural. Instead, I look as our dog does when she hopes to avoid a
scolding, her head cocked to one side, her forehead wrinkled in
anxiety.

"If you make a face and the wind changes, it will stick." My
grandmother tells me this when I am very young. I believe
her—I believe everything she tells me—and I worry: What if
I am inside the house and I make a face not knowing that it's
windy outside? My face could be frozen forever in a grimace,
or a look of surprise, my mouth a round O that I would never
be able to close. I resolve to arrange my features into a pleas-
antly neutral expression and keep them that way, so as to defeat
the unseen wind. But, no, this will never work. I can't remain
conscious of what my face is doing for even a minute.

A winter morning, a Saturday. I am no longer a child but a
woman of thirty, and my grandmother is ninety-one. Still, her
power is such that I remember all her pronouncements: that if
I were to step on a needle it would travel through my blood-
stream and pierce my heart; that if I cross my eyes too many
times they won't uncross; that opening an umbrella inside the
house or putting shoes on a table invites disastrously bad luck;
that there are cases of people who never stop hiccupping and
some of them die. I don't believe any of these, not quite, but I
don't forget them, either. And her cautionary tales about snail

fever turn out to be legitimate. Schistosomiasis is a parasitic disease, but you can't catch it from garden snails, only from freshwater ones; the disease belongs to the Third World, in which she did grow up.

Standing in the hall outside her bathroom, I watch as she readies herself for a trip to her hairdresser and then on to the supermarket, where each week we walk slowly through the long aisles and she picks among the food and groceries, squandering as many minutes as she can on each choice: among brands of crackers; boxes of dry cereal; patterns printed on rolls of paper towels. It's her only outing of the week and she looks forward to it, and to having my undivided attention for as long as my patience lasts. Still in her housecoat and slippers, she's looking at her reflection in the mirror. She doesn't know I'm there, as I've paused in the shadows, and am silent.

Outside the window, snow is on the ground, and light falls on the tiled floor in long blue-white bars. My grandmother is so small and bent that the mirrored door to the medicine cabinet can't show her any more of herself than her face, and she looks at it for some moments, holding herself straight so that her chin makes it into the mirror's frame.

She doesn't see me in the hall outside the bathroom door: She doesn't know I'm watching her. Slowly, she reaches forward over the sink and touches her reflection. "I've grown old," she says, speaking to no one. "Suddenly, I've grown so old." There's wonder in her voice, mystification: How has she failed to notice what must have been happening for some time?

It's a private moment, or I might move to comfort her. I might try to distract her from it. I might make tea or suggest we sit by a window where we can watch the people on the sidewalk as they pass before our house. These are among her favorite pastimes, making and drinking tea, watching strangers as they go about their business.

But it's not a moment I can enter, only one I can destroy by intruding. I retreat up the stairs. I've seen the arrival of my grandmother's awareness of her death, its imminence. I won't forget what I've seen; I will carry it forward. It will become part of my apprehension of my own mortality, a thing so certain and unavoidable and even so natural that I imagine myself standing, one of an infinite line of women, generations going forward as well as backward. As if my grandmother or I, any one of us, were caught and multiplied between opposing mirrors, I see all of us reach forward to touch this harbinger of our deaths—the face, once a maiden's, now a crone's—trying to understand what we can't understand, because how can Being grasp Nonbeing? How do we practice feeling it, the absence of ourselves?

One day I look into my bathroom mirror and find that the person I expected to see isn't there: She's disappeared. This moment is divided by years from the day I watched my grandmother confront her reflection. I am now thirty-seven, my grandmother no longer living.

And they are connected.

More seriously depressed than I admit or even perceive, only a day away from what I don't anticipate—a stay in a psychiatric hospital—not sleeping or eating, unable to work or think straight, I've gotten into the habit of comforting myself with a photograph that reminds me who I am, who I used to be. It's a snapshot my husband took. I'm sitting with our two older children in a field of summer wildflowers, all of us bathed in light that looks genuinely golden, light that is a benediction. We're smiling; the wind lifts my son's pale hair into a halo. I use this picture to call me back into myself, reorient me to what is the essence of my life. It works well, too, until suddenly it doesn't work at all.

The children are in school, my husband at work. I look at the photograph and don't recognize anyone in it. *Who are these people?* I think. *Who are they to me?* I wait for the image to take effect, to reach past whatever is wrong with me, but nothing changes. I know I'm supposed to know them, *us,* but they're no different from the people who come flattened under the glass of a newly purchased picture frame, a set of smiling strangers whose likeness you're meant to discard and replace with a picture of your own.

I put my snapshot away in the drawer, walk into the bathroom, and stand before the mirror, staring. Apparently it's possible, from one day to the next, from one hour to another, to slip out of one's skin, one's self, and land in a new, alien, and unrecognizable face.

Time passes, months, then years, and that bathroom mirror loses its power to frighten me. Still, I find it mysterious, and even wonderful, that there would be so stark and irrefutable—so apt—a symptom of nervous breakdown as a failure to recognize one's own face.

"Look," my husband says. "That's not her face. Her nose isn't that short, and her mouth doesn't look like that. And the eyes are the right size but not the right shape, not exactly." We're discussing a piece of art made by our older daughter, soon off to the Rhode Island School of Design—where she will paint, very well. It's a life-size self-portrait, the final project for a course in advanced drawing. I think it's very accomplished, I tell him. Especially I like the placement of the figure in the frame, and the way she's rendered her hands, which, I point out, are difficult.

But my husband sees a problem: Our daughter, he concludes, has fallen prey to an idea of how she looks, and this idea is different from how she really looks. We continue to talk, about the drawing, about magazines and TV and movies, and how media may influence, even create, our daughter's idea of her face. Perhaps she can't see her face clearly, surrounded by a society so eager to tell her how she's supposed to look—to define the contours of a perfect face, to direct attention to certain details over others, to make one face an icon, another unworthy of notice.

The idea stays with me long after our conversation ends. Each of us must see his or her physical self through a lens of various influences: prescriptive advertisements; critical remarks from parents or siblings or lovers; the human tendency to conflate physiognomy and character, mistaking a high forehead for intelligence or full lips for sensuality. Perhaps when we are young and enthralled by the faces of certain models or actors, we're affected by something beyond their looks. We assume, of course, that powers are granted them by celebrity and imagine these might belong to us if only we looked as they do. But perhaps the psychic trajectory is more complicated.

Couldn't it be that we project what we wish were true of ourselves onto the faces of famous strangers, finding heroism, self-confidence, dignity, genius—whatever qualities we aspire to possess—in the way they appear? Don't we mistake their faces for illustrations of what we desire in ourselves? Don't we try to emulate what we see, or begin to believe we look a little like these more nearly perfect avatars, these faces of who we might, with effort and time, become?

And wasn't this what I lost or inadvertently broke ten years earlier, when I didn't recognize myself: my idea of who I was, who I am. That lens of influences and aspirations, whatever apparatus would have guided my self-portrait: I must have lost what allowed me to bring myself into focus.

Sometimes I'm startled by the face I see reflected back at me. Not the countenance I review each morning, unfolded from sleep, washed and subjected to quick analysis, to moisturizer, tweezers, and whatever corrections I can effect with cosmetics. That face is little more than a list of tasks to accomplish: teeth to brush and floss, brows to check for stray hairs, under-eye circles to mask with concealer, lips and lids and lashes to color. I'm speaking rather of the face I see inadvertently, cast back at me in a shop window as I hurry through errands. Who is that woman? Whose dark and angled glance meets my eye in a department store mirror I don't anticipate? She looks to be a solitary soul, the face who catches me unaware; she looks anxious and driven. A face I glimpse rather than see.

I catch her; she flees—the right-hand me with the hooded eye, the face I thought I banished and summoned at will, using her to silence garrulous fellow travelers or defend me against the occasional boor. Apparently she isn't obedient but emerges according to her own agenda, knifing efficiently through sidewalk crowds, both punctual and eager to avoid the touch of strangers.

And me. As much me as the left-hand self with her wide, dreamy eye, the self I own more readily because she's attractive, flirtatious, quick to smile, to laugh. The lines she's traced on my face are lines I like, radiating out from each eye. Different from what the right-hand woman has etched into my forehead.

Perhaps the unseen wind did change one storm-tossed day when, heedless of the consequences, I was looking as I felt: dark and brooding, overcast by fears. That face stuck, and others did as well—the one, for example, I wore when sitting in a field of wildflowers, golden. My grandmother didn't say I'd have only one face. She didn't say it couldn't happen again and again with every shift in the wind. That was my misunderstanding.

The Book of My Body

I'M STANDING, NAKED, ON A CUBE OF A PLATFORM IN A MAN-hattan photographer's studio. It's a late afternoon in January, rush hour, but outside his shuttered windows traffic is moving slowly, its usual clamor muffled by a heavy snowfall. Months before bikini season, my pubic triangle is beach-ready, not a hair out of place. I got it waxed three days ago, just to be sure that any redness that resulted would have faded by now. These are color shots, life-size.

"Can you turn your right knee farther out?" the photographer asks me. "I need to get all the inner thigh. Good, good—that's great. Perfect. Okay, now we'll do the back."

I turn around to face a blank white wall. The room is comfortably warm, especially where I am, under two umbrella lights.

"You really have to spread your legs wide for these. If you move your feet all the way to the edges of the—right, that's the way." I hear the wheels of the stool the photographer is perched on roll toward me over the white floor. He must be about eye-

level with my buttocks, a word that's always sounded aggressively muscular to me, certainly more than my own would
merit. The flash keeps popping; the directions keep coming;
the lens ascends my body, bit by bit.

"Wow," he says when we're done. He thrusts his hand forward to shake mine. "You were excellent."

"Really?" I say, surprised.

"Really," chimes in the woman whose job it has been to
chaperone this session.

Chaperone was how the photographer described her when I
made an appointment with him. I'd asked if there was anything I needed to know in advance of our session. Not really,
he told me, but I might feel better if I was aware from the out-
set that there would be a chaperone present. I laughed and told
him it hadn't occurred to me that I'd need one. A legal precaution, he said.

"What made me any better than average?" I ask, curious as
to what might be the criteria for an excellent subject. Just as I
know that I have been not nude but *naked* for these photographs, I know the assessment cannot be aesthetic. Nudity has
all the advantages of art: good lighting; cosmetic adjustments
before the fact, airbrushing and sundry technological tweaks
after; poses and postures and expressions that presume an ob-
server who appreciates beauty. I, on the other hand, have only
this: Before we began, the photographer stuck ten centimeters'
worth of an adhesive-backed tape measure to my flank, in
order to demonstrate accuracy of scale.

"Oh, you know." He smiles. "No crying, no screaming."

"No fainting. No running away," the chaperone adds.

"You're kidding," I say.

"I wish," he says.

"He's not," she says. "He's telling God's truth."

They leave me to peel off my ten centimeters and note the red welt the adhesive leaves. I put on my clothes alone. Dressing, unlike being naked, is private.

As promised, the book of my body arrives in three weeks, via FedEx. It cost me a lot of money, this book, and it is mine to look at as much as I want, which is not at all. I give it to my dermatologist and ask that she keep it in my file.

"It really is for you," she says, "to use at home between appointments." She's paging through the black binder and making little noises of delight, as if turning through a rare monograph of her favorite artist's work. Which, it occurs to me, she probably is. "Oh, this is fabulous," she tells me. "I'm so happy you got this."

"Me, too," I say. And I am, as long as I don't have to look at it.

For years my dermatologist had been pressing me to have documentary photographs made—by a specialist in medical photography—so that she would have the means to track tiny changes in my skin. While her memory of my epidermis is extraordinary, she is, after all, human. A life-size, blindingly lit, and mercilessly focused material record makes it easier to do her job, which is to find skin cancers and remove them before they remove me. I wasn't yet twenty-five when first diagnosed with skin cancer, not the "good" kind that doesn't kill you, but the bad kind that can.

"I really want you to keep the book here, at your office," I tell my doctor. "Please?" She nods, too engrossed by the nape of my neck to answer.

I don't want to look at it too closely. I am determined to preserve my innocence of these images, which document every last millimeter of my forty-five-year-old epidermis and its many imperfections—the apotheosis of the "warts and all" school of portraiture.

Included among what I do not want to see are: age spots; crow's-feet; skin tags; cellulite; those funny little red spots that multiply as we "mature"; a few areas that after the births of three children didn't snap exactly back to their prepregnancy tone; the perennially dry wrinkles around my elbows; myriad little surgery scars—the removal of suspect imperfections; the slackening of the skin on my neck; a couple of wrinkles I find particularly objectionable; and all the dorsal moles I can't see well enough to compare to their pictures anyway. These last alone seem like a good enough rationalization for entrusting the book to my doctor, whom I see—who *sees* me—every six months.

At her uptown office, its waiting room populated almost exclusively by women pursuing state-of-the-art means of disguising their age, I strip in a back room and am examined, minutely, *every*where. I rarely get away unscathed, and it is this particular physician's scrupulousness, her proclivity to cut first in order that a pathologist can ask questions later, that ensures my remaining faithful to her, despite the fact that she is not in my medical plan. For her I pay out of pocket, and through the nose. Her caution is the necessary antidote to the foolishness of my youth, when I didn't yet believe in cancer or in death, and when my taste was about as sophisticated as Malibu Barbie's. As a teen, I spent all summer every summer in the Southern California sun, whitening my very long blond hair with lemon juice, and basting my skin with Hawaiian Tropic's dark tanning oil. By September, when school reconvened, I was bronzed to perfection. Except for the pink tip of my nose, which had blistered and scabbed over more times than I bothered to count. And there was that one second-degree burn on my chest the year I turned fifteen, blisters the size of halved oranges, sobering, if a bit late.

A few months after my mother died of cancer, I took my grandmother to the dermatologist for a routine exam. As long as I was there, I asked him to look at a mole on my chest. It was a very dark mole but it wasn't irregularly shaped or even unattractive, and he said not to worry about it. He was a preeminent doctor, a famous one, actually, and this is what he said: "It's nothing."

"But I don't want it," I told him. And I didn't. Admittedly, I had conceived an irrational dislike for this particular mole. "I wish you'd just take it off," I said. He shrugged, and indulged the request. Two days later he called to inform me it had been a malignant melanoma and that he was scheduling me for outpatient surgery. More tissue would have to be excised from around the small, casual hole he'd covered with a Band-Aid.

"But," I said, "isn't . . . aren't those the bad kind? The kind that can, um, metastasize and kill you?" I was twenty-four; that I might have skin cancer hadn't occurred to me.

"Yes," he said, and hung up, a man with great credentials and no bedside manner. He didn't even acknowledge his mistake, let alone apologize for telling me he'd misjudged a potentially deadly lesion. I guess he was avoiding any admission of malpractice, which hadn't occured to me, not then. I faulted him for being impolite and insensitive.

The doctor who performed the second surgery left a scar big enough to invite curiosity. The diagnosis underscored my precocious fear of death, which had grown along with my mother's cancer until it reached a proportion that alienated me from my young peers. I was the only twenty-four-year-old I knew who fretted continually about how little time she had left. One melanoma predicted not only future lesions on my skin, but raised the possibility of getting one inside an eye. While the malignancy that was removed hadn't been invasive, it didn't guarantee that no cancer cells had escaped. The era of vigilance had officially begun. Suddenly I was among the nervous ranks anticipating the milestone of five years without a recurrence. What had been a cosmetic choice was now a medical one. Without consulting with me, my dermatologist excises whatever she finds suspect. In ten years as her patient, I've had only two malignancies: an incipient melanoma that she excised from my temple—it was tiny—and a basal carcinoma on my forehead: less tiny than vanity would have liked.

Because foreheads are not very fleshy, and because the lesion was in so obvious a place, my dermatologist referred me to a specialist in what's known as Mohs surgery, a process that spares as much benign tissue as possible. For a small, relatively minor operation, Mohs surgery takes a long time. The surgeon lifts a first layer of cells from the site and, instead of closing the wound, passes the layer to a technician. The technician immediately prepares a frozen biopsy slide for a waiting pathologist, who reports either that the surgeon has taken enough or that he must go down to the next layer, and so forth. Once the surgeon has reached purely benign tissue, he reconstructs the hole he's left, very gracefully in my case, which required only three biopsies. Six months later, the scar, aligned with what the surgeon tactfully called a "natural facial crease," is virtually invisible, even without makeup.

"Don't you mean wrinkle?" I said from under the scalpel, and he smiled.

"Now, now," he soothed. He was a good fifteen years younger than I, handsome and clearly practiced in making diplomatic concessions to the self-esteem of middle-aged women. As for me, I don't require flattery. Survival is the main issue. I'm always so relieved—ecstatic—to have been spared, thus far, the fulfillment of my gruesome fantasies of metastatic brain cancer and eyeball tumors and weepy deathbed scenes with the children I haven't yet raised.

"See you soon," the receptionist trilled after the follow-up exam for the carcinoma surgery. I heard her cheery goodbye over and over for the next few days. *They expect me back,* I kept thinking, they expect me to need future surgeries. That chipper little call and wave provided the necessary psychic pressure to make an appointment to get what my dermatologist had been asking for: the book of my body.

I see a page now and then, by accident. My doctor holds it open in her arms as she looks at me. She wears a visor with a magnifying lens as she scrutinizes first me and then the relevant picture. Eyes closed, relaxed under the thoroughness and competence of her search, it suddenly occurs to me: Assuming the book does its job, the reason for my avoiding the sight of my forty-five-year-old skin will change. One day, God willing, I won't want to be confronted by images of a smoother, more supple self. It will pain me, this irrefutable evidence of youth.

By Angels' Speech and Tongue

I'm trudging up Taylor, in San Francisco, a street so steep it has concrete stairs in place of a conventional sidewalk. The unusually deep treads make the ascent awkward; to avoid falling I have to keep my eyes on my feet instead of where I'm headed. At the top of Nob Hill waits the labyrinth inside Grace Cathedral, another walk requiring downcast eyes, lest one stray from its narrow path.

I don't know what, if anything, I'm expecting from the experience.

Though I haven't set out to find her on this abbreviated pilgrimage, conceived to fill a business trip's unscheduled hour, already my mother, dead for twenty years, is slipping through my thoughts, as dark and expressionless as a silhouette, taunting me with her opacity. How foolish to have imagined her death might release me, or that I might enter a church without her at my side. Sunday was the only day of the week I could expect to see my mother, the hour of mass the single one I dependably shared with her when I was growing up. I never paid attention to the liturgy, my attention fixed on the remote young woman at my side.

Within me is the other kind of labyrinth, like the trap Daedalus designed to stymie the Minotaur and contain his rage. I haven't yet learned that I, not the one who has injured me, am the person who suffers my withholding forgiveness.

I traded one of the boys next door three of my Hot Wheels for the breastplate from his knight costume. I already had a scimitar made of hard plastic painted to look like chrome, with a jeweled handle. It was a pirate's sword, but I used it to play Joan of Arc. It was a good game for an only child, because the real Joan of Arc's companions were invisible to other people, too. I used the round lid of a metal trash can for a shield. I did not use the hobbyhorse because it was stupid all by itself, and worse under Joan of Arc.

By the time Joan was seventeen and had proclaimed herself the virgin warrior sent by God to deliver France from her enemies, she had been obeying the counsel of angels for five years. The voices she heard, speaking from over her right shoulder and accompanied by a great light, had been hers alone, a rapturous secret. But in 1428, when the angels pressed her to undertake the quest for which they had been preparing her, they transformed a seemingly undistinguished peasant into a visionary heroine who defied every limitation placed on a woman of the late Middle Ages.

At God's behest, Joan ran away from home, sheared off her hair, and dressed herself in male clothing. She nagged at her uncle, who lived in Burey, a village near her hometown of

Domrémy, until he agreed to take her to Vaucouleurs. She had been visited by angels, she told him, and they had directed her to speak with Robert de Baudricourt, the captain stationed there. Baudricourt, the angels said, would provide her the means of getting to Chinon, where the French dauphin had taken refuge following the English occupation of Paris. But when he learned what the peculiar girl wanted of him, and what authority she claimed, Baudricourt told Joan's uncle to give her a sound thrashing and take her back to her parents.

Joan would not be dissuaded; she returned twice more to Vaucouleurs, inspiring enough gossip and curiosity that Baudricourt asked a local priest to perform an exorcism to be sure Joan wasn't keeping company with demons rather than angels. The priest's judgment that there was no evil in the girl, her claim that she and no other could save France, and the captain's desire to end her months' long campaign for his support convinced Baudricourt to provide Joan an escort to Chinon. The journey through enemy territory took eleven days on horseback and concluded without so much as a skirmish. Once Joan had at last penetrated the French court, she presented Charles, the fainthearted dauphin, with a private miracle, one that neither ever revealed. Whatever it was, it convinced the dauphin that Joan was in truth heaven-sent, it was God's will that he wear France's crown, and it was she who must lead what was left of his army to recapture all the territory the English had annexed.

Given a warhorse, armor, and some five thousand soldiers, Joan took up her sword. She was frightened of the enormity of what God asked of her, and she was feverish in her determination to succeed at what was by anyone's measure a preposterous mission. And yet she roused an exhausted, underequipped, and impotent army into a fervor that carried it from one unlikely victory to the next. Most famously, she turned the tide of the Hundred Years' War when she saved the city of Orléans from the English by defying the cautious strategies of seasoned generals to follow inaudible directions from invisible beings.

By their "speech and tongue," she told the inquisitors who sent her to the stake. That's how she knew they were angels.

Perhaps it's a small thing I don't want to lose, or maybe I think of it as currency. In either case, I keep it in my wallet's zippered pocket. There was no occasion warranting a gift, and I remember she said I was too old to beg and wheedle and make a scene. A woman made of painted wood with hair as dark as hers, smiling and round under her red dress and apron: a mother, clearly. The wood squeaked when I twisted the halves apart. Nesting dolls, seven of her, one inside another, ever smaller and rendered with less detail until the smallest's face had room for only dot eyes and a mouth like an eyelash. That was the only one I'd wanted, really, the seamless kernel that didn't come apart in my hands.

I wonder now if my attachment to that most rudimentary incarnation, fetal in its lack of distinguishing features, was a way of wishing myself back inside her, the larger dolls a series of wombs, one giving birth to another. Imagine the safety of a child so protected.

What did it feel like to be my mother? The question dogs my heels, turns each corner with me as I slowly approach the labyrinth's center. I'm convinced that if I knew what she hid from me—if I knew her—I'd have what I needed to banish her.

———

By angels' speech and tongue. It was during her thirteenth year, Joan of Arc testified under oath, that she first received what she described as "a voice from God to help her and guide her." The voice came on a summer's day, when she was in her father's garden. As it was noon, the church bell was ringing, but Joan hadn't even the chance to cross herself before the garden vanished, and the sky and the earth as well. No river, no houses, no green pastures with their white spatter of sheep. There was nothing but light, "a great deal of light on all sides, as was most fitting," she told her examiner, reminding him tartly, "Not all the light came to him alone!"

The voice's arrival was of consuming interest to Joan's inquisitors. How could it not have been? Over and over they questioned her in the attempt to access, or construct, evidence that might be used to prove the voice's source demonic. But all it had given Joan on that first afternoon was the kind of mild direction a clergyman might extend to any child. "Be good," it had said, and "go to church often."

After the voice had fallen silent and the garden emerged from the flood of light, Joan found herself "much afraid." The visitation preoccupied her; already it had slipped between her and the life she used to have. For the remaining seven of her nineteen years, Joan's daily companions, whose company she chose before that of mortals, and whom she obeyed as she did not any mortal, were angels. Asked if she believed she had sinned in leaving home against her mother and father's wishes, Joan answered that had she a hundred parents or been the daughter of a king, she would have left nonetheless. Whatever she did, she insisted, was at the command of God.

The clergy couldn't tolerate Joan's belief that she had access to God outside the authority of the Church—outside their control.

Still, it wasn't Joan's inquisitors who led her to the pyre. It was her angels.

I'm irritated by other people on the path, whispering together or wandering off before reaching the labyrinth's center. Even more, I'm irritated with myself, always chasing—like my mother—after whatever elusive mystery that, once penetrated, might reveal life's purpose. My mother was born a Jew and indoctrinated as a Christian Scientist, converted to Catholicism, orbited through Transcendental Meditation and into the gardens of Los Angeles's Self-Realization Fellowship only to, in the end, return to Catholicism. She watched TV evangelists on her deathbed, and hid scraps of paper bearing a Buddhist chant—*Nam Myōhō Renge Kyō*—under her pillow and in her purse. When will I stop following in her wake, sifting compulsively through life's details to find the one where God is hiding? I should be outside, taking pleasure in one of San Francisco's rare sunny afternoons, instead of advancing a few steps, only to turn back on myself in a twisted circle.

It's easy to dismiss Joan's voices, to reduce them to a symptom and her life to a case study. The judges to whom we commend Joan are doctors of medicine rather than the church. She's been handed retroactive diagnoses of hysteria, schizophrenia, epilepsy, even tuberculosis.

Academics don't judge; they interpret. Feminist scholars posit a Joan calculating enough to costume herself as a visionary, like Saint Catherine of Siena or Saint Bridget of Norway, during an era when mystical revelation was one of the few routes a woman might take to political power. Cultural anthropology reminds us that it is during times of overwhelming social crises—like that of fifteenth-century France, staggering in the wake of war and plague and famine—that visionaries arise. Ethnographers identify shamanic figures as a feature of successful societies; granted passage to states of consciousness that elude most of us, they are the repository of our fears and hopes as well as our means of petitioning the divine. Neurotheology has discovered a "God spot" in the human brain; four out of five people experience feelings they identify as rapture when specific areas of their temporal lobes are stimulated by a magnetic field. If the brain is wired for faith in a higher being, it must be that faith conveys an evolutionary advantage.

"The first maker of the gods," William James wrote, "was fear."

One foot in front of the other. The path is too narrow to accommodate more than one person at a time, and so we wind on, single-file, a sparse and straggling queue of supplicants. Halfway through the maze, I've yet to free my thoughts from workaday cares and reproach myself for failing to arrive at anything resembling a meditative state. What is this emptying-one's-mind business? I can't even slow my thoughts down, let alone exile them.

Abruptly, a voice comes not from above but from all around me, its volume one of magnitude more than sound. Later, when I try to remember the voice, I'll think of dancing in front of speakers at a rock concert and feeling sound too loud to hear, feeling how my bones vibrated within their envelope of flesh. It's a terrible analogy; I can't do better. The few people walking the labyrinth, the nun sitting in the pew by the exit, the sacristan replacing candle stubs with fresh tapers: Not one of them looks up. They haven't heard a thing other than the careful tread of feet or the clicking of rosary beads.

You want to know? the voice demands, and its tone chastises. It tells me I've asked and asked and asked again, like a whining child, for something from which I have been protected, for knowledge withheld to spare me pain. *I'll give you what you think you want.*

Even as the voice falls silent, I'm stricken with a fear worse than any I have ever known or imagined. Depthless, black, and cold, it crowds my chest, pushing everything aside. Fear makes me nothing but chest. No brain with which to reason, no legs to carry me away, no hands to shove it away. Only a pair of lungs that have forgotten how to inhale. I stop moving long enough that the clicking rosary, having grown weary of waiting behind me, steps off the path, and reenters a few paces farther ahead.

The primary aspect of a mystical state is ineffability. "It defies expression," James tells us. "No adequate report of its contents can be given in words."

As Joan's trial for heresy progressed, so did her descriptions of the voice or voices that guided her. The more she was pressed to describe what couldn't be described, the more fully she characterized it as angelic, in that it conveyed messages from God. A single voice accompanied by a great light became a trio of voices that could be distinguished from one another, those of the archangel Michael and the virgin martyrs Saint Catherine and Saint Margaret, all widely venerated at the time. The voices conjured beings with lips to speak, bodies she could see and touch and even smell, creatures with wings and crowns.

A few of Joan's biographers attribute this embellishment to desperation. The months of the trial's public sessions were followed by more months of private interrogation in the dank cell where Joan spent the better part of a year, shackled to her bed, threatened officially with torture, unofficially with rape. As it was believed that the devil could have no commerce with a virgin, her persecutors had motive enough to establish that Joan was not, as she claimed, inviolate, penetrated only by female hands searching to ascertain the truth. Against protocol, she was guarded not by women but by men, who had opportunities to rape her. When she asked for a confessor, she was given a false one, whose instuctions were to extract information for the inquisitors.

Who was it who persuaded her to have angels with their arms, feet, legs, and robes painted on the standard she carried into battle? her judges wanted to know. She "had them painted in the fashion in which they were painted in churches," she said.

It's typical for mystical visitations to accrue definition and detail. Joan had had an experience, thousands of them, in fact, that required explanation. What if her sojourn among French royalty, passing through castles and cathedrals filled with religious paintings and tapestries accomplished under the court's patronage, gave her an idiom with which to explain her voices? Familiar figures, holy and God-sent, they could have provided the vessels in which she could safeguard what she didn't want to forget or deny, rapture so overwhelming and potentially disorienting that it required containment.

Did she herself ever see them in the manner in which she

had them painted? Joan refused to answer. Under no circumstances would she disclose her visions and revelations. As demonstrated by the trial record, no amount of threats could force her tongue. "Truly," she said to the judges when they showed her the rack that waited for her, "if you were to tear me limb from limb and separate my soul from my body, I would not tell you anything more: and if I did say anything, I should afterwards declare that you had compelled me to say it by force."

So this is what she hid from me, the monumental goddess of my youth, at whose feet I fell. How is it possible to live with fear like this? How did my mother carry it, putting one foot in front of the other? It's primal, almost animal—the inarticulate fear of a child lost in a crowd, blind with panic, groping for a familiar hand. The fear of annihilation.

When she was a child my mother lost three beloved governesses, one after the other; with each she had an intimacy surpassing that which she had with her mother. By the time I was born, there wasn't any money for a governess. I claimed more of my grandmother's attention than my mother ever had. How many times had I asked myself the question: What happens to a child who loses one mother after another?

Epiphany. A manifestation of the divine. Is this what I've been given, reluctant, naysaying Catholic that I am? That my child mother—and how much younger she grows as I age— was afraid, not fearful but broken by fear; it doesn't answer to every hurt, but it explains enough. I don't need to twist her apart anymore so I might look inside.

Stopped in my tracks, my eyes cast down to hide the tears that drip from my nose and make dark circles on the stone underfoot. Reduced by panic to begging, my prayers are barely coherent. All I can muster is some version of *Take it away, take it away, please please take it away. I understand now, take it away.*

As it is: The fear lifts. But not before it has settled into me, teaching me, in as much as I can be taught, what it felt like to be my mother.

Later, I won't be able to remember what happened during the remainder of the afternoon. I won't know if I completed the labyrinth, or if I, too, wandered away, annoying those who remained on its path. I suppose I sat in a pew to gather my wits before going to whatever appointment waited. Or maybe I canceled it. Maybe I just went back to my hotel.

I can still picture the too-deep stairs on Taylor Street and revisit my irritation with how awkward they made the climb on the way to the church, but I don't remember walking back down.

How was she sure from the beginning that the source of her voices was divine? Joan said she "had the will to believe it."

Child that I am of an age when plagues are caused by germs and not God's wrath, and the divine right of kings has yielded to the election of presidents, I want not to believe. As soon as I characterize what I heard as having issued from beyond my own consciousness, I begin arguing against the possibility of its being so. My objections are, of course, entirely reasonable. That's just what's wrong with them.

It's courage that Joan is remembered for, her selfless physical courage in battle and, even more, the courage of her convictions. She had the audacity—some would say the insanity—to defy dozens of Sorbonne-trained judges who intended to put her to death. As for Joan, she preferred death to a life in which she betrayed those she loved most. That she was sure she was bound for paradise was considered a heretical presumption.

On May 30, 1431, Joan of Arc, nineteen years old, was led to a pyre built upon a high platform, so the jeering crowd, an estimated ten thousand people, could watch her burn. But among even the English, who sent her to her death, there were many who succumbed to "great weeping and tears" and "made professions of faith" before the spectacle was concluded. After, the executioner went to the Dominican convent. "He greatly feared he was damned," he told his confessor, for he knew "he had burned a saint." Joan died nobly, her dignity unassailable, praying and calling on Christ before she finally expired. Like Christ, she asked for God's mercy on those who had persecuted her.

While aspects of Joan's life will always be beyond our power to understand, her courage is not among them. Its magnitude reflects that of her faith.

Another gift from my mother, a necklace, lost for so long now I'm surprised I can picture it so clearly. A fine gold chain bearing a glass orb the size of a cherrystone. Within it was a single yellow mustard seed suspended in a drop of glycerin.

So I had it once, and could carry it with me: the measure of faith enough to move a mountain.

Mini-Me

THE CONVERSATION ALWAYS ENDED WITH MY HUSBAND STAR-ing, as he tends to do when he has run out of things to say, at the blank white page of the ceiling, his head resting heavily on the back of the couch. Sometimes I waited for him to make a definitive pronouncement; more often I got up and wandered into the kitchen. It was never a fight, but a question I'd been raising and my husband deflecting for years. I wanted a third child, and the line we'd drawn marking the possibility of blight visited on a woman's aging eggs drew ever closer until, suddenly, it was in sight: my fortieth birthday.

Wasn't it greedy to ask? Wouldn't we be punished, my husband suggested, by having to accept whatever portion of misery might be visited on the parents of two healthy, intelligent, and attractive offspring who petitioned God or the gods or just plain luck for another? "It's not as if," he added, revealing a heretofore-hidden streak of superstition, "we have two boys or two girls and are holding out for the unrepresented gender."

The point didn't dissuade but provoked me in its symmetry. Let's shake things up, I thought. Let's get uneven, let's have a baby. I wanted one, I wanted one, I just did, and when I pointed out that it wasn't as if he'd felt ready to have either of the first two, my husband was politic enough not to challenge me. We both knew there was no discouraging this desire.

Our daughter was five and our son three when I began my campaign. If anyone had asked me to articulate my insistence on a third child, would I have admitted the reason? Did I know it in the moment? I wanted emotional insurance. I didn't imagine myself a woman who would soar once her nest was empty. What I foresaw was closer to a plunge. If we had a third, when the older ones went off to college I'd still have a middle-schooler, and by the time that child went to college I might have at least the hope of a grandchild.

My husband reminded me of the cost of raising children, not just financial but psychic. Would we have the time and energy to give a third as much as we had the first two? Maybe more, I argued. By the time the third arrived, the others would be so much older, almost a set of junior parents; I wouldn't have to divide my attention between two young children. My husband reiterated his fear that having "already won the lottery," as he referred to our having been blessed with the two children we had, if we asked for another we might be punished by the fates. I relayed his superstition to the doctor who had delivered our first two children.

"Are you kidding?" he said. He leaned forward over his desk, having just told me I was "perfect and beautiful," which might sound creepy, given the assessment followed his having peered, minutes before, at what neither I nor my husband had ever seen. But he was an obstetrician; the beauty he saw was fertility. A couple who had had two healthy babies was that much more likely to have a third healthy child.

"But I'd be so many years older this time around," I said.

He smiled. "That's what amnio is for."

"Wow," friends said when they ran into me on the street, and they said "Congratu—" but most of them never finished the word before silently doing the math and arriving at a different one: *accident*. They kept their eyes averted, seemingly stuck on my swollen midriff. I could have rescued them. "Oh, no," I could have said. "She was planned." But I liked watching them struggle with the presumed faux pas, their discomfort announcing that in the eyes of the world, this pregnancy was different from the earlier two. And it was, but not in ways I could have anticipated.

"Don't underestimate the power of a negative role model," my analyst had said when I was pregnant with our first child and struggling with my fear of being less than the good-enough mother. Every dream we dismantled together was a nightmare. My mother moved through them like a vampire, pale and deadly. "You were supposed to ransom me," she told me when I was thirteen, reporting epiphanies from her own sessions with a therapist. "Another daughter to give my mother, to replace me so I could escape." I don't remember a time when I didn't know that all she wanted and didn't have—college, career, husband—I had taken from her. She made me understand from the start that I had stolen any hope she had of happiness.

My grandmother accepted the ransom; her vicious battles with my mother ceased; the house grew calm; I thought I would die of grief. The person I wanted before any other didn't want me. Years of psychoanalysis couldn't deliver me from what I understood as a fall from grace, stranding me in the purgatory of unrequited love, from which I was determined to escape. Love is given, of course, not earned, but I couldn't turn away from the red taillights of her turquoise Pontiac, always sliding away from me down my grandparents' long driveway. I looked for opportunities to prove myself worthy of love. If I could distract her from the form I'd assumed—an unwanted burden, a cross to bear—she'd see I'd eclipsed that unsatisfactory girl with a new, radically improved me.

It didn't work, of course. Nor did her death, when I was twenty-four, release me from the habit of attempting to woo her. For a decade already I'd been the emblematic anorexic, precocious in my grade-school discovery of mortification of the flesh, punishing parts of my body before I set myself against the whole. I was the good girl who got straight A's, the high school valedictorian who hadn't had a drink, much less sex, before she landed in college, the woman who never found a way to escape the long-reflexive habit of always becoming and never being, perpetually striving to evolve.

Shoved by therapy, I arrived at the familiar truism: It hadn't been me who was unlovable; my mother, a child herself when I was born, had been unable to love.

The arrival of our firstborn stripped me of the defenses I'd painstakingly acquired, and to which I paid lip service. Now I knew what only childbirth could have taught me. I belonged to the life I'd summoned into being; I was my daughter's as much as she was mine; the bond was irrevocable. How—it did not seem possible; I couldn't get my head around it—*how* could a woman let go of her child? All through the year in which I carried my daughter in my arms, and the one in which she toddled and spoke, and the next, when I dropped her off at nursery school while carrying her baby brother on my hip: Over and over motherhood returned me to a place that looked a lot like the land of the unrequited. Only this time I was a mother, not a child. Had there been something wrong with me after all, a thing that made me different from my children, lacking the power to command a mother's devotion?

Long summer afternoons at the beach segued into picking pumpkins and making Halloween costumes. When winter held us indoors, we visited the dinosaurs at the Museum of Natural History, or stayed home to bake cookies. One art project at a time, my older children destroyed the mahogany dining table at which I'd done years' worth of homework, never marring the finish because I knew better than to defy my grandmother's dictum to cover its surface with its thick, custom-made pad before laying so much as a pencil on it. I loved playing with my children; I enjoyed their company as I did no one else's; and I loved ruining that beautiful table, eventually replacing it and the memories it carried with one I liked better, one on which we spilt milk—and paint, and glue— without crying over it. But all this happiness inspired an equally unexpected emotion: resentment. Before I had children of my own I hadn't known, exactly, what I'd missed. Now I saw it, and what I saw sharpened my grief, and my anger.

And then came the longed-for third, my husband having chivalrously joined me in what hadn't been his idea, even if he did try to claim credit the moment our third child was in his arms.

But three, not four: That was the bargain, and immediately upon her birth I had a tubal ligation, the one form of contraception that redefined menopause. The third would be the last, and I marked her first words and first steps with the awareness that I was bidding these goodbye, forever, even as I added them to the sepia-toned gallery in my head. I saved one bottle of breast milk at the back of the freezer, hidden under an ancient bag of frozen peas, and from time to time I'd take it out to feel what preserved it, hold that chill tight in my hand. Years passed; the bottle remained under the peas; my younger daughter grew. Nursery school. First grade. Chapter books. Once again, the Tooth Fairy secreted a cache of golden Sacagawea dollars in my desk drawer, way at the back. Before they were spent, our older children were in college, and I had a ten-year-old who was, of course, far more than who or what I'd fantasized.

What would I do without a child in the house? Because I was firmly in my role—as firmly as I could humanly be—of the good mother, or at the very least the good-enough mother. Bath time followed by bedtime; eating green vegetables; not chasing balls into the street. A lot of it was common sense, I discovered, and Dr. Spock, who remained on my nightstand for decades, provided further counsel. I didn't have a positive role model to apply to ambiguous situations, but I did have a formula. Or maybe *reflex* is a better word for my rule of thumb: Given a choice, I followed a course opposite to that of my mother. Whenever I needed reassurance, I resurrected the child I had been to consider the situation from her point of view. By the time our third arrived, I'd navigated a decade of childrearing and had two bright, happy, confident children—apparently the formula worked. Was it all right to allow my daughter to wear her Sleeping Beauty costume when it wasn't Halloween?

To wear it on the street for months, ever more tattered under its detergent-defying stains? I didn't care, I decided, if the dirty acetate ball gown inspired equally dirty looks. My daughter, five years old, never saw them. She was looking in shop windows to see herself, the girl the prince was going to marry because she was beautiful and good.

No, I wasn't ready, not at all, to stop serving the paragon of maternal virtue I'd constructed to rebuke my mother. If I couldn't, in my thirties, articulate to myself what emotional insurance might mean, by the time our third was in grade school, hindsight revealed me as a woman who had assembled her adult self around the persona of the good mother, the inverse-reverse-opposite of mine. I didn't want an empty nest, because I wasn't sure I was whole enough to survive without a child at home.

"Mini-Me," one of my students called her, when circumstances forced our younger daughter to tag along to class. And it was true: Our childhood photographs are as interchangeable as our baby pictures. The words stuck in my head; I couldn't banish them. Mini me. I worried that our physical similarity might heighten the risk of conflating my daughter with my child self, especially as it was that child self on whom I depended to illuminate my children's needs, and I was vigilant with our youngest, who upped every ante.

Once, I caught my fifteen-year-old daughter rolling her eyes at the worshipful gaze her little sister—then in kindergarten—kept locked on me. "Once upon a time," I said, "you used to think I was the cat's pajamas, too."

"Yeah, but I was never your stalker."

I didn't argue. Her little sister might not have loved me more than she or her brother did, but she did do it differently. As though the golden fluid the amnio technician had drawn from my womb had bathed our daughter for nine months in a distillate of longing, she answered my desire with a single-minded passion for me, holding a mirror to not only my face but also my personality—a deeper and more threatening reflection that, in the case of my little doppelgänger, I wanted to avoid. But how could I, when I recognized my daughter's hunger as my own? Could it have been that the ravenous desire I turned on my mother wasn't purely a matter of nurture but one of nature, a trait bestowed by genetics? If I saw a friend on the street, my daughter marched me in the opposite direction, so intent on preventing even a wave hello that whoever it was laughed. When I tried to ignore her interruptions while I was on the phone, she unplugged it. If I looked away, she took my face in her hands and redirected my gaze.

Eerily, as if following a script I'd bequeathed her, she acted out scenes that had unfolded decades before she was born. She came to me while I was sleeping and pried my eyes open with her fingers, as I had done to my mother before she moved out. Once I was up, she insinuated herself between me and my clothes, me and the coffeepot, me and the newspaper. For years, she made sure I never closed the bathroom door when she wasn't on my side of it. What would I have done, I wondered, if the third had come first? I'd needed a decade of practice to navigate the third sis's demands with the grace I expected of myself.

And I'd needed something only a doppelganger could have given me—a way to cast off the resentment inspired by my attachment to my older children, to stop asking why love hadn't held my mother hostage and kept her by my side. Under eyes as predatory as the ones I'd fixed on my mother, I found myself no longer able, or even inclined, to judge her. My third child taught me what it was to want to extricate myself from her hot little embrace, put her down, and bolt. Sometimes, held captive, I'd feel my heart hammering in my chest, the kind of acceleration inspired by a stuck elevator: claustrophobia segueing into panic. But among the advantages I had and my mother didn't was this: The little girl in my arms was so familiar in her needs I never had to guess at them, as I sometimes had had to do with her sister and brother.

I knew when it was okay to unwrap her arms from around my neck, pull her legs from around my waist, set her down, and take a break. And I knew when I had to count to ten, or fifty; I knew when separation would feel like punishment, just as I knew, before obvious symptoms arrived, when any of our children was falling sick. When a good-night kiss wasn't enough, I left my husband as the lone host of a dinner party. If a plan with a friend fell on a night I couldn't leave without inspiring desperate tears, I canceled it. My daughter saved invitations to functions I told her I wouldn't attend because I'd have much more fun at home, with her. She added each to her collection with a radiant, triumphant smile. And yes, I allowed her to open my sleeping eyes with her fingers, because I remembered what it did to me when my mother pushed me away.

In the dream, my mother is eighteen. One of the handful I'll never forget, it unfolds in a hospital room, impersonal, utilitarian, a bed that goes up and down. She's sitting up between the two sets of chrome bed rails with a baby curled on her chest, not a new baby, one of maybe six months, and she looks so tired. I'm watching her from the hall outside her room, standing where she can't see me. I know she's exhausted, unequal to taking care of the baby and too ashamed to complain.

"Here, let me take her—you look so tired," I say, coming into the room.

She doesn't speak; she just hands the baby to me, lifts her gently off her chest—the baby is dressed in a long-sleeved onesie made of red calico with little flowers all over—and as she hands her to me, our eyes meet. I can see that she is grateful, and there is something in her gratitude toward me, for taking the baby off her hands, that causes each of us anguish.

The picture of me at fifty, my older children in college, my youngest at home, was recast by our third child. She was at once the easiest child, in that I understood her so well, and the most difficult, rarely satisfied by anything less than my undivided attention. Would I have leaped so eagerly into motherhood a third time had I known that my own mother, eighteen years old and terrified of the baby in her arms, would greet me, summoned by a granddaughter she never met? I'd wanted to eat my mother alive, to possess every last little bit of her. I wanted so much more than I ever got, and losing her as I did would always inspire grief. But now it wasn't so much for me as for my mother, whom I forgave without trying, my rancor like a pulled tooth. I kept looking for it, just as I'd feel, with my tongue, for that missing part of me.

I had the means, now, to reinterpret if not rewrite history. Had I been my mother, I might have left me, too. And the speed with which my taillights disappeared down the driveway wouldn't have proved a lack of love. All it would have meant was that I'd been unequal to staying; the misery on my face wouldn't reflect my disappointment with my child, wouldn't betray a lack of affection, but instead how torn I was, how divided against myself.

Pilgrim's Progress

THE TWELVE OF US ARE TO GATHER BETWEEN 11:00 A.M. AND
1:00 P.M. at the big red cow on the lower level of terminal 2D
of Paris's Charles de Gaulle Airport. We've been assured that
the big red cow is impossible to miss, placed as it is in the center of *l'espace boutiquaire*. It's barely dawn; the line at border
control moves with the near inertia of the morbidly sleep-
deprived. After what I mistake as an amiable welcome from the
officer who stamps my passport, I ask if the terminals are connected by *un chemin de fer*—a railroad—and summon the extravagantly pained wince the French reserve for Americans'
syntactical missteps.

"*Il n'y pas un train,*" he says through his nose. Slit-eyed, he
slides my passport back under the bulletproof window. I know
the word *train,* but I expect the French to complicate matters,
and my reflexive response to an identical cognate is to reject it
as too easy. When I ask how to get to terminal 2D, the officer
says nothing. Instead, he shakes his head, closes his eyes, and

exhales loudly, audibly forcing air from his nostrils. Dismissed, my own head hanging too low for me to note the multilingual instructions above, I unintentionally drift from my prescribed exit lane and call down yet more French opprobrium.

Baggage pickup, toilets, ground transportation, first aid, lost and found: I see signs pointing the ways to everything but terminal 2D—pointing to every terminal other than 2D. The woman at the information desk under the outsize blue *i* has a genial expression. Still, as if I've arrived in first grade rather than Paris, I take the precaution of singing the French alphabet silently to myself, just to be sure: In French *d* is pronounced *day*.

"*Où est le terminal 2D?*"

"*Ici.*"

"*Ici?*"

"*Oui,*" she says, and shifts to English. "This is terminal 2D." She throws open her arms and smiles with something that looks like pride, as though introducing me to a vista of unsurpassed beauty. "You are standing in it."

"But . . ." I close my mouth. I was sure my flight terminated in 4B, but there's little to be gained by telling her how I came by this misinformation—on Air France's website—so I nod, I thank her, I step away from the counter that separates us.

As it turns out, even more apparent than the cow—which is shiny, like an automobile, and gleams evilly under fluorescent light—is that the subterranean *espace* I am approaching does not in any measure fulfill the fantasies I spun around *boutiquaire* while suffering the pinched and folded misery of a sleepless red-eye. My imagined *espace* was crammed with actual boutiques whose merchandise betrayed a subtle yet discernibly fabulous chic impossible to acquire in the United States. The bookstall sold all the magazines I'd foolishly resisted buying before boarding the plane in New York. A café plucked from the Latin Quarter served exemplary coffee and croissants on round marble tables set before comfortable wicker bistro chairs; a vast skylight floated overhead. My *espace* was an ideal setting for a pleasant transitional interlude between my early-morning landing and my midday rendezvous with eleven other Joan of Arc enthusiasts, some of whom are bound to be, like me, fanatics.

In the real world, there isn't a bookstall, only a sparse food court, a rental-car counter, and a drugstore, where I spend a surprising number of euros on Visine, ibuprofen, and a newspaper. With a cup of coffee that suggests fast food is not improved by being French, I begin my frustrated search for somewhere to sit. I make a slow lap around the cow, which stands in the middle of a raised flower bed filled with one of those hardy plants that thrive on artificial light. The cow itself, approaching the size of a panel truck, is puzzling. It isn't art and it isn't advertising; it doesn't appear to reference cheese. What it is, is an impediment to surveillance. There's no perch both far enough from the cow that I'm not in danger of being identified as one of the twelve and near enough to spy the others before they spy me. Every angle is interrupted by vast, glistening red flanks. I could leave and come back at noon, but I'm too tired to hunt down a less dreary spot. So I just sit in a molded plastic seat in the food court and contemplate the nausea particular to drinking coffee on an empty stomach. What do they look like, Joan of Arc fanatics? I scan the clots of passersby, the plan to spend my time productively by galvanizing my rusty French via reading *Le Monde* revealed as an ambitious conceit.

Weeks before we were to assemble in Paris, all but one of us filled out questionnaires addressing our respective values, goals, and hobbies. I don't have any hobbies, which people seem to find suspect, and I hate trying to come up with something that won't crack under the pressure of scrutiny to reveal otherwise hidden aspects of my being. I wrote down yoga and beachcombing, one a daily practice, the other an occasional diversion, neither of which I consider a hobby, and which together suggest a calm repose I have never experienced. The group leaders—I'll call them *M. et Mme. les Directeurs,* or *M. et Mme.* for short—circulated our answers, as well as their own, via email. *M.,* an American, and *Mme.,* his French wife, belong to a mega-church in the South, and sign correspondence with "Blessings." Now, too late, it occurs to me that what they've called a "pilgrimage" rather than a "tour" must have an agenda, our trajectory through France an exercise in proselytizing designed to deliver us, at its conclusion, to a greater appreciation for Jesus as well as Joan. Our packing instructions did suggest we bring soap and a Bible.

M. et Mme. sent a picture of themselves smiling widely and standing before one of the sites we'd be visiting. They asked for our photographs in return, but they didn't share them among the group, so I don't know what a self-confessed member of an international role-playing community inspired by *Star Wars* looks like, but I do know how to say his name because he sent us all a recording of its correct pronunciation. One woman thought to inquire if the monasteries in which we would be staying had a dress code. She's probably not wearing a habit, but I've involuntarily conceived one for her. It's circa-1975, with a knee-length, navy-blue A-line skirt, half-wimple, and black sensible shoes, and I can't separate it from her any more than I can Luke Skywalker's tunic from the role-player, whose name has but two syllables and sounds just as it looks. I know the state trooper is tall and burly with sandy hair, because he introduced himself to me two months ago at a reading in Manhattan. When I asked how he'd found me he said he'd background-checked everyone who'd signed on for the pilgrimage. Naturally, I am afraid of him. Because I never think to do things like that—not even to google *M. et Mme. les Directeurs* before sending them a check for a substantial amount of money, all that was left of my research budget for a biography of Joan of Arc—family and friends have concluded that I am impractical at best. And when not at my best, an unfortunate combination of credulous and impulsive.

I'd never before considered traveling with anyone while working, but I couldn't afford to make the trip I'd envisioned, requiring a car and up to three weeks' worth of lodging and meals. So I searched "Joan of Arc tourism" and happened upon *M. et Mme.*'s site. Their efficient itinerary and monastic accommodations would save me time and money, and—more important—release me from foreign car rentals and the panic of getting lost. Because I always get lost. Under the spell of my iPhone's dizzying little screen, I have been adrift for an hour in a single square mile of Brooklyn, whereas *M. et Mme.* had traveled the route over and over, as many as a dozen times. Experience would have taught them the way from one site to the next as well as a sustainable pace, whereas history predicted I would accelerate into driving all night so as to avoid wasting daylight hours in the car—and/or compensate for having gotten extravagantly lost—only to arrive at what I'd look back on as reckless decisions, often with rueful effects. I need ballast.

Aside from *M. et Mme.*, the role-player (who is in fact wearing a tunic, if not one from a galaxy far, far away), the woman in the post–Vatican II habit, and the trooper, I need: a self-described free-spirited poetess; the curator of an extensive collection of Joan of Arc memorabilia; a wispy-haired, wild-eyed Bulgarian on her third or perhaps fourth Joan pilgrimage; an amateur historian and his horticulturalist wife; and a peculiar, slouching sort of man with greased-back hair—the only one of us who didn't fill out a questionnaire and the lone adult on the lower level of terminal 2D I do not for an instant consider a potential pilgrim because he is obviously a serial killer.

There are two rented vehicles. *M.* drives the van that holds eight people; *Mme.* takes the sedan. I note, as the bags are loaded, that I was alone in slavishly hewing to their no-bigger-than-17x10x10-inch rule. I always pack soap; I did not bring a Bible or enough clothes. My carry-on is filled mostly with books, as I apologize to *M.* when he winces while lifting it into the back of the van. *M.* is a slight man, afflicted with what my grandmother called a "poisoned" toe, requiring adaptive footwear.

Reflexively avoiding the larger group, I hang back and get the passenger seat of *Mme.*'s sedan. To be fair, the state trooper should have this roomier spot; instead he is folded up in the rear, next to the curator. We can't trade places, as I offer to do, because once *Mme.* learns I read French she decides I will relieve her of the burden of watching for important signs, allowing her to concentrate on the driving. The responsibility of navigation is rendered considerably less terrifying by the car's GPS, its oral directions inflected with the same synthetic calm in French as in English. Too, as *Mme.* explains, *M. et Mme.* communicate on the road by "talkie-walkies."

"Ees eet walkie-talkie?" she asks mildly in response to my stifled laugh. But *Mme.* doesn't take offense. The talkie-walkies have about a half-mile range, and their use inspires frequent roadside map conferences. We never do get lost, we are never even on the verge of getting lost, but *Mme.* is so convinced we will that she cannot be satisfied merely by years of experience and a global positioning device. As *M.* later observes, *Mme.* is a nervous type, and he is patient about pulling over as many times as necessary to reassure her that we are on course.

Whichever vehicle we chose for the first leg of the trip is the one in which we will make the whole of it, because to abandon one set of traveling companions for another is not only inherently insulting but, as every seat in each vehicle is taken, would force a trade, so no one does. By means of these fortuitous social dynamics, I get the best seat in the less populous car while also avoiding what talkie-walkie background chatter suggests is the more pious atmosphere of the van. Consumed as she is by the earthbound demands of driving, *Mme.* has no ambitions of tackling the infinite, and in this context, at least, tolerates our descent into secular discourse. She is a psychiatric nurse with very good posture. I imagine she's suspicious of pleasure. Petite, pretty without effort, crisply tidy in her windbreaker and sneakers, *Mme.* is what her countrymen would call *correcte*.

The first stop on the pilgrimage, Rouen, is the city in which Joan died. For reasons of efficiency, we don't follow her footsteps in order, which might prove disorienting if I didn't know her life backward and forward, as do several of the other pilgrims. With the possible exception of the serial killer, each of us has read at least one biography of Joan, and even the serial killer must know the basics.

We reach Rouen in the afternoon, too late to explore the city proper but allowing us time to settle into our accommodations at a monastery in the exurbs. *M. et Mme.* strike me as excessively chipper as they spring out from behind their respective steering wheels, but they've been in France for a few days already; the rest of us are dazed in the wake of overnight flights. While we idle at a locked iron gate, *M. et Mme.* gain entry to the building through a secret passage around the corner. Fewer than five minutes pass before I turn my suitcase over on what isn't a sidewalk but the edge of a road. I sit on its side, feeling the stacked books beneath me, sturdy as a bench. It can't be an hour but it feels that long before *M. et Mme.* return to lead us, tilting forward and dragging our possessions up a gravel incline to the monastery's official entrance. There we are dispatched to our separate rooms.

We never see the nuns who live in the monasteries that accommodate our group; they exist only in what evidence they leave behind: the meals they lay out for us, the linens at the feet of our beds. In return, we pilgrims remove all traces of ourselves, washing dishes and replacing them in the cupboards, making the beds on arrival and stripping them on our departure. My first room comes with an extra chore. A nun's firm hand has left directions on a placard framed like a photograph and set on an unvarnished desk: After showering, guests are to use the cleanser and sponge in the blue plastic bucket to clean the tiled stall. I pull aside the curtain, which is too narrow, certain to allow water to spill onto the linoleum floor. I reach up to redirect the showerhead away from the opening, but it doesn't budge. The obvious strategy is to shower as quickly as possible, using my body to block as much spray as I can, and then to dry myself and mop the floor with the dish-towel-size rectangle of rough terry cloth. I decide to wait for morning.

These invisible nuns unnerve me. A twist of atavistic logic suggests that because I can't see them they must have secreted themselves to watch me, waiting to see if I scrub the stall. I lie on my bed—an uneven set of springs under a sponge mattress thin enough to roll up like a carpet—and suffer an epiphany. While I don't disapprove of mortification of the flesh, I never imagine it as petty domestic torment. My mortification fantasies are tainted by glamour and excitement. There is never linoleum or bad linen. It's not something I can or want to change about myself.

At dinner the serial killer turns out to be a scientist whose face I'll remember as disconcertingly shiny. He says he works in a laboratory, and his clothes convey institutional regulation—military minus regalia. Also, they are Brownshirt brown. We're gathered around a refectory table listening to a Jesuit imported for our edification. Many Japanese come to Rouen to pay tribute to Joan, the Jesuit tells us. They see her as a female samurai. Notebook open, I try to strain potentially useful information from his lecture, but my attention is compromised by my efforts to discern how much the sisters have watered down the wine.

Something happens the next morning, before we head into the city of Roven, and it will happen the subsequent morning and all the ones after, and it will grow steadily more excruciating. At nine we are called to assemble in a small meeting room next to the refectory. There *M.* introduces us to what he calls *Question du Jour,* a topic to be addressed together each day before we set out in pursuit of a girl who lived six centuries ago. As Joan's career is the inspiration for the questions, all are religious in nature and—to my mind—fiercely intrusive, demanding I relinquish intimate details of my relationship with whatever I imagine God might be. The inaugural inquiry, concerning how Jesus might speak to those of us who don't hear the voices of angels, is enough to separate the sheep from the goats. The trooper, the serial killer, the curator, and the amateur historian and his horticulturalist wife don't show up for a second *Question du Jour.* I am among those who do—not without discomfort.

Having started her life on the wrong foot, my teenage mother grew up a seeker of elusive truths, and I, her only child, tagged behind her through one religion after another in hopes of securing her attention. Pickled as I am in doctrines, as far as I know I have never been saved; perhaps I am unsalvageable. For nearly thirty years, ever since my mother's death and my estrangement from my preacher father, I've limited my exposure to organized religion, and avoided those who betrayed missionary urges. But I know that boycotting the *Question* would precipitate a fall from *M. et Mme.*'s good graces, which would be ill advised. I might wish to turn to them in the future as liaison to one of the Johannic scholars they have searched out in the course of their tours.

I try to give only brief and general answers, yet, finding myself incapable of addressing matters of faith dishonestly, I tell the truth, which, being the truth, does not set me free but strips me bare, nails me to my chair with embarrassment, and unexpectedly extracts a daily tithe of tears. This new species of mortification is compounded each morning by my growing certainty that *M.*, the Bulgarian, and the role-player believe my weeping is inspired by the arrival of the Holy Spirit. I can tell they think they're watching someone being reborn by the way they leer excitedly at me, as if I were a baby taking its first steps. I feel thoroughly violated. And one tear begets two, and two begets three, and on it goes, a biblical flood. Once I start it's hard to stop.

The twelve of us, a hushed and solemn flock of disciples, follow the expert guide *M. et Mme.* have engaged to lead us through the narrow cobbled lanes of old Rouen. Streets laid out during the Middle Ages are curved to prevent an enemy from seeing down the length of them, the expert tells us, and people did not, contrary to popular opinion, empty their chamber pots out of their windows and onto passersby. "This is a lie," she says, and she looks at us as if the idea were a piece of New World slander.

We pause at the wall surrounding the archbishop's palace, where Joan was found guilty of heresy and witchcraft. The expert walks us through the tower where Joan was kept under brutal guard, and she gives us an hour to explore what was once Saint Ouen's cemetery, where Joan received a public sermon on her wickedness and from which she was taken to the old market, where death awaited her. Now the cemetery is a garden, and the old market is dominated by a modern church, whose architecture strikes a discordant note among its medieval neighbors. A cross marks the place where Joan, nineteen years old, was burned at the stake. It's a simple monument, underwhelming. I wish it were an eternal charred circle, and that I could kneel to rest my hand on it.

Uninterested in the contemporary church and cross, I return to the tower, to linger alone where Joan was kept for the last six months of her life. I want to walk without the others through the cobbled alley where Joan hobbled in chains, escorted, day after day, from prison to courtroom and back again. As he will for the rest of the trip, the trooper tails me.

"I can tell you're the kind of person who gets lost," he says companionably on the way to rejoin the others, and I follow his lead. In truth, I'm not quite clear on where *M. et Mme.* parked the van and car.

The monastery where we stay the longest is laid out like a school dormitory, with a dank linoleum corridor illuminated by a fifteen-watt bulb—but only for the ten seconds after the front door is opened; then the light snaps off. As my room is toward the end of the corridor, I learn to enter the building, key in hand, and sprint to my cell and unlock it. Otherwise, I have to feel my way back and start over. The communal shower is outfitted with Lilliputian towels and insufficient hot water, lacking the pressure to rinse shampooed hair before running cold. Every morning, I wake up, put on yoga tights and tank top, and sit on my lumpen cot, from which I stare at the wall and fail to summon the will to stretch out my spine. Perhaps, even as inconvenience and discomfort push the Bulgarian and the role-player up the Hill of Difficulty and on to the Celestial City, I am sinking into the Slough of Despond.

The trooper has. Unwittingly, he sentenced himself to two

weeks of relentlessly bad food—*in France*. Who could predict such a thing? Breakfast is weak coffee, bread, and jam. With the exception of one luncheon, the midday meal is unmemorable enough to be forgotten immediately. Dinner is always frozen quiche, strangely dense and of low stature, its source clearly an institutional food service. Sometimes tiny pink cubes of ham are discernible under its pale surface. There is a salad of iceberg lettuce, carrot shavings, and wan sliced tomatoes glistening with oil and vinegar, but no dessert.

Invariably, the wine is watered.

Mme. is usually silent during *Question du Jour,* but when we broach the topic of the source of Joan's strength, she leans forward in her chair and says that faith is like a muscle. If we fail to cultivate it, it atrophies. She looks quite ferocious as she says this, her accent suddenly sharper. She raises a clenched fist to make her dainty bicep pop, and her vehemence lifts her to her feet. I've never experienced atrophying faith, nor do I possess the ability to either cultivate or neglect it. For me faith arrives violently and then, having had me in its teeth for a spell, drops me like limp and bloodied prey. Whether in the throes of its advent or departure, I try to keep all evidence of it hidden, as I would an unsightly wound.

The monastery in Joan of Arc's birthplace doesn't board, only feeds pilgrims, so in Domrémy we stay in a *gîte* owned by "Robert." *M. et Mme.* are on friendly business terms with Robert, who has provided rooms for their pilgrims before, but his jovial lack of interest in religion and their disapproval of that are equally evident. He sells wine out of the back of his car and swears there is a ghost in the main house, which has settled in a room allegedly used by Napoleon III for assignations with a mistress.

The Bulgarian has begun wearing a dress made of not-quite-white string, possibly crocheted, like a wedding gown assembled from a great number of doilies. Maybe it is inspired by her preoccupation with the idea of mystical marriage to Jesus. As many times as possible she attends mass in the chapel next door to Joan's childhood home. I suspect that when alone she prostrates herself before the altar, facedown and arms out. She and the *Star Wars* role-player, a serious young man bound for the priesthood, fall to their knees whenever an opportunity presents itself. Both are given to long, contemplative walks. The role-player corrects me, erroneously, on the few occasions I speak about Joan, who called herself *la Pucelle*—the virgin. It shouldn't annoy me as much as it does that a man who sent us a recording of the correct utterance of his name incorrectly pronounces *pucelle,* with a soft Italian *c,* the kind in *cello,* rather than the sibilant French *c* of *ice*—just as it shouldn't fill me with such delight when, while following a path Joan once walked, he is chased by an enraged cow.

From Domrémy we make field trips to other places in Lorraine, including Vaucouleurs, from which Joan set out on her quest to lift the siege of Orléans, and Greux, where her mother grew up. One day we ascend a mountain to partake of a feast hosted by the Prince and Princess of something, whose pileup of *du*s and *de la*s atop *van der*s and *von*s exhausts the ear before the affixes at last deliver it to the patronymic. Royals in street clothes are inherently disappointing, but this couple does live within what was once a genuine medieval castle, its ruins not so ruined that they don't offer a sense of what castle life might have been like. The site, chosen for its elevation, allows for a 360-degree panorama of the farms and fields spread out below, and we spend an hour wandering the periphery of its tumbled stone walls and keeps.

M. dogs my steps, inasmuch as his poisoned toe permits. What is my "slant"? he wants to know. I understand the question but pretend I don't, to stall for time.

"My slant?"

M. nods. "Your slant on Joan. For your book."

I know what I am supposed to say, but instead I say, "I guess I'm hoping to avoid slants."

I can see from M.'s expression that this is an unwelcome piece of news, this attempt to remain upright and unslanted, especially after such floods of seemingly reborn emotion.

The *Du-de-la-van-der-vons* lead us to their home, built within the ruins' embrace, and, after an aperitif, usher us to a banquet table. Curiously, the prince and princess have no servants and, unlike the nuns, wait on us in plain sight. After the first course, when no table maid appears to clear the plates, I rise to help the princess, who presses me back into my seat, her hand exerting considerable downward force on my shoulder.

There are many courses, each accompanied by its own wine, and it is not long before conversation—*M. et Mme.* and I translating the *Du-de-la-van-der-vons'* comments—turns to topics typically proscribed under such circumstances: politics, money, and sex, in that order. The upcoming election will fix nothing, Prince *Du-de-la-van-der-von* says, and the princess agrees, adding that the general economic downturn is the result of *homosexualité,* not a word I can soften through export. *M. et Mme.* nod emphatically, and I glance at the overtly gay curator before turning to the princess.

"Je ne savais pas princesses étaient tel fait accompli," I say, realizing too late that in my wine-addled fluster I substituted *fait* for *chefs.* She smiles at me over the pear tart.

At the conclusion of an exhaustingly bibulous meal, Prince *Du-de-la-van-der-von* leads us to his distillery. Lorraine is known for its mirabelles—small yellow plums whose sweet juice is distilled into wine and liqueur. The prince points at his highly polished copper still and beams at us, announcing that it was he who made the dessert wine we drank minutes earlier. *"Oui, oui, oui, je suis le vigneron!"* he says, his cheeks aflame with his product.

It's not until I find myself in the attached gift shop, with its castle etchings and castle tea cozies and bottled mirabelle wine, that I realize what everyone else undoubtedly understood all along: The *Du-de-la-van-der-vons* are a professional prince and princess, their previously mystifying delight in entertaining us something we purchased. I buy a castle blueprint, a practical acquisition.

Taken in the context of my weeping during *Question du Jour,* I worry that spending evenings alone in my room might suggest I am on my knees, consumed by solitary prayer, rather than working on my book. Usually, I'm typing up the day's notes or annotating the record of the inquisitorial trial that sent Joan to the stake or—with increasing frequency—staring at the ceiling while lying on the floor in hopes of minimizing the damage done by monastery pallets to the pinched nerve in my neck.

My French is good enough that I can follow fluent conversation, but only with effort. I never travel with a camera, not while doing research; it forces me to look carefully at what I might otherwise miss. By evening I've remained sufficiently focused and engaged to leave me speechless with fatigue.

Every night I fall asleep contemplating what has become for me the real *question du jour,* to which I return, helplessly: *Am I going to cry again tomorrow?* I'm pretty certain that if the Holy Spirit were the catalyst of my weeping, there would be some joy in it. One morning I try answering with my eyes closed, to make my fellow pilgrims disappear, but still their stares peel back my skin, scour what's underneath.

To enhance our experience of Reims, *M. et Mme.* have engaged an elderly art historian as our guide to the cathedral to which Joan led the Dauphin Charles to be crowned. The man is both learned and charming, but before he's even halfway through the tour, *Mme.* tries to cut it short. We are expected at the monastery for dinner at seven, she says; we must leave now to be on time.

"But it's only just five," I say, and *Mme.* flattens her lips into a line.

The free-spirited poetess protests, too, and the Bulgarian joins the mutiny. The trooper follows suit. Realizing that the two factions are at an impasse, staring at one another with crossed arms, the guide steps forward and offers to drive the insurgents back to the monastery at the end of the visit.

"Do you know how to get there?" *Mme.* asks, ever concerned with the prospect of getting lost. He shrugs.

"Everyone knows how to get there," he says.

Mme. leaves, quickening her stride to catch up to *M.,* who, in consideration of his ailing toe, took a head start to the van with the rest of the pilgrims.

"But first," the art historian says, after we've made a luxuriously thorough examination of the exterior's renowned bas-reliefs, "I must return home briefly. For the keys," he explains. "It is not far."

In fact, it's literally in the shadow of the cathedral. "Also," he says, "I must feed my cat." The cat requires an unexpectedly lengthy spell of attention, but the sun is still up when the historian reappears. "Hmm," he says, when he turns the key in the ignition and it makes a little click, followed by silence. He turns it again. "Dead," he says unnecessarily. The trooper asks if the historian carries jumper cables, which the elderly gentleman hears as "jumper stables" and, before we can derail him, embarks on an equine line of inquiry.

"Oh no," he says of the idea of attaching his car battery to another. "This is a dangerous practice." The trooper's recital of his military service and police career, each requiring expert training in many dangerous practices, does nothing to allay the historian's apprehensions. "In any case, we do not have such wires here," the man says, seeming to imply all of France in his argument.

After a friendly exchange of addresses we will never use, the four of us wayward pilgrims set off in search of a taxi, which proves a lengthy quest. By the time we are en route, it is half past seven. Sitting in the backseat, the poetess and I look at each other and recognize our mutual fear of *Mme.*'s certain wrath and start to cry.

As we arrive and head up the now dark entryway, we can

see our fellow pilgrims on the other side of the refectory windows, silently raising and lowering their forks as though on an illuminated stage. All heads turn our way as we open the door. By now I've had to pee for so long that I can't think of anything else, and I head directly for the washroom, where I splash cold water on my face before taking a seat at the table.

Is it my imagination, or are *M. et Mme.* disappointed as well as disapproving? If we were to be late, I suspect they would prefer us to turn up even later, our hunger greeted by nothing but washed plates. The poetess glares at me so furiously that under other circumstances I'd have been unable to eat. As it is, I'm so hungry I just keep my eyes on my quiche. No wine at all this time.

"How could you!" the poetess says when we are alone at the sink, washing and drying, immersing ourselves in menial atonement.

"What did I do?"

"Making me go to her alone!"

"Mme.?"

"I had to apologize all by myself." She almost stamps a foot. Her blue eyes spill. "You should have been with me!"

"I had to go to the bathroom," I say. "Besides, I didn't know we were going to apologize."

"What did you think we were going to do?"

"I don't know. Just, you know, sit silently and eat in a penitent manner."

The poetess thinks I'm lying. Before we left the cathedral, I asked her and the others to wait so I could use the women's room, but I never even looked for it. Instead, I went back to where Joan once stood, during the coronation of Charles VII, and I knelt to place my hands on the stone floor that was once under her feet. I'd rather the poetess think me a liar than tell her the truth.

All twelve of us attend our final morning meeting, which is not a *Question* but an opportunity to share our impressions of the pilgrimage. I say I'm grateful to have visited places I'd previously known only secondhand, through books or movies, a comment echoed by several others. When it's *M.*'s turn, he says he has observed that we are all trusting people. "You had no idea who we were," he says of himself and *Mme.,* who nods vigorously beside him, "and you came along on this journey trusting us with your lives."

Upon investigation, it turns out that I alone am so trusting, at least by the measure *M.* chose. It wasn't just the trooper: Everyone else did as much googling as possible. This fact, validated by the hot blush accompanying my confession of such guilelessness, invites comparisons to the simple faith of children and reinstates me in the favor of *M. et Mme.,* inspiring an impromptu climax to our last formal gathering.

Because I have embarked on such important work in writing a biography of Joan of Arc, it would be a wonderful thing, *M.* says, for us to pray together for my success.

"You don't mind, do you?" he asks, then goes to fetch someone who turns out to be the mother superior.

I do mind. I mind very much. I mind enough that my pulse knocks against my eardrums and my jaw locks. The idea of it inspires the kind of horror that attends nightmares of discovering, too late, that one has unwittingly gone to school naked.

But really, I try to assure myself, how bad could it be, how long could it take?

Very, and forever.

"Praying together" requires me to kneel before a wimpled, whiskery, emphatically visible old nun, who drops her heavy hand on my bowed head, inciting all the other pilgrims to lay their hands on my person. Every atom of my being cringes under the touch of uninvited invocation. Eyes closed, I recognize the role-player's clammy fingers. Frozen quiche and uneven mattress coils, hair shirts and scourges: Such trials are no match for this mortification, which burns me through, scalds my cheeks with blazing tears. The prayers begin in French and trend into English, their purpose to unbalance and slant, at which they succeed, but only inasmuch as I sometimes suffer vertigo when overtaxed. At one point I'm so close to being physically ill that my mouth floods with saliva. And when it's over, it doesn't stop—only replays in my mind, filling me with unchristian feelings.

We take leave of one another at a restaurant near the airport hotel, most of us bound for early-morning flights. The Bulgarian hands out prayer cards. The poetess and I slip ours between the pages of our notebooks, the serial killer leaves his on the table, and the curator regards his with what looks like weariness before sliding it under a basket of bread. The trooper is too busy with his *bifteck* to pay any heed. "It was tough," he says later. "But at least it was meat."

Back in my room, I consider digging my wrinkled pajamas from the bottom of the carry-on, but it's not worth the trouble

of repacking everything as cleverly and tightly as the bag's unreasonable size demands, so I end up sleeping naked, and thus
poorly, caught in an exhausting cycle of short dreams of falling,
jerked back into consciousness at the conclusion of each. In the
morning I'm only more tired, which must explain my forgetting the international prohibition against carrying jars of exotic
regional mustards on a plane, along with honey made by bees
that graze the Veuve Clicquot Champagne vineyards.

   "Ils ne sont pas des liquides ou des gels," I say uselessly. What is
it about petite French women in crisply pressed navy-blue uniforms? This one has a military-style hat with a sharp little prow
in lieu of a brim; it projects considerable authority. I suspect she
knows this, as she punctuates her sentences with quick, jabbing
nods.

   "Vous ne pouvez pas les prendre dans l'avion."

   "Mais—"

   "Mais non."

The offending jars, lined up on the counter between us, are
each swaddled in an unwashed sock, to prevent breakage. The
agent pulls on gloves to disrobe them. She shakes her head.
"You cannot leave them," she says, switching to English.
"These you cannot get anywhere but here." I wonder if she'd
summon this level of protective vehemence for Spanish olive
oil or Ligurian pesto.

   "What do I do?" I ask. The prim uniform looks at me, hat
cocked, then at my little condimental ambassadors for France.

   "You will check them," she says. I make it a point never to
check anything, as I hate extending the misery of a long flight
with a subsequent detention at the baggage carousel, all the
while anxious to stake my place in the taxi queue.

   "But I have nothing to put them in," I say; and after a sharp exchange with the sharp navy-blue hat to her left, the agent steps sharply out from behind the counter.

"You will come with me," she says, jabbing, and I do, half expecting to be delivered into the hands of the *police de l'aéroport*.

Ten hours hence, I'm standing on the lower level of terminal 1 of JFK, waiting for the dark portal feeding the conveyor belt to disgorge my forcibly (and expensively) packed box of bubble-wrapped jars. It's the very last thing off the plane, and I watch as it slowly turns the corner and approaches me. The suddenly sinister-looking brown cardboard box draws the attention of a police officer and his K-9 unit German shepherd, whose scrutiny so unnerves me that I fail to claim the package on its initial orbit. And so it goes around once more.

I'd be less cautious had I not convinced myself that I'm presently on a terrorist watchlist, due to an incident two weeks before, when I was flying to Paris. On that evening, as I walked through security, an alarm sounded, and I remembered a lighter I'd inadvertently left in my back pocket. I took it out to surrender it, and the TSA agent stepped back, saying, "Take it easy there, ma'am," and told me to put my hands over my head.

"I don't even smoke." I said this as if it might mitigate my crime. And I don't—the last thing I'd done before leaving for the airport was to light a votive candle bearing an image of Joan of Arc, for the success of the trip I was embarking on. I didn't say a prayer, but after the little flame jumped up, I took a minute to watch it burn before I blew it out.

Acknowledgments

The author wishes to thank Hillary Black, Anne Burt, Liz Farrell, Christina Baker Kline, Lori Leibovich, Kate Medina, Cathleen Medwick, Beth Pearson, Anna Pitoniak, Joyce Ravid, Michael Ray, Deborah Seigel, Ilena Silverman, Annette Szlachta, Amanda Urban, Daphne Uviller, and Catherine Wolff.

Publication History

The essays in this book were originally published in different form in the following journals and anthologies:

"A Tale of Two Dogs": *Zoetrope: All-Story,* Spring 2010

"Keeping Vigil": *More,* September 2005, and subsequently in *I Married My Mother-in-Law: And Other Tales of In-laws We Can't Live With—and Can't Live Without,* edited by Ilena Silverman (New York: Riverhead Books, 2006)

"True Crime": *More,* October 2013

"Holiday Lies": originally published as "Was That You, Santa?" in *The New York Times,* December 18, 2009

"The Couch Account": originally published as "Count the Ways" in *The Secret Currency of Love: The Unabashed Truth About Women, Money, and Relationships,* edited by Hilary Black (New York: William Morrow, 2009)

"The Forest of Memory": *Salmagundi,* Fall 2006, and subsequently in *Only Child: Writers on the Singular Joys and Solitary Sorrows of Growing Up Solo,* edited by Deborah Siegel and Daphne Uviller (New York: Harmony Books, 2006); *More,* February 2007; and *Truth in Nonfiction: Essays,* edited by David Lazar (Iowa City, IA: University of Iowa Press, 2008)

"Cat Fancy": *Zoetrope: All-Story,* Fall 2006

"Baby New Year": originally published as "Cradle to Grave" in *Self,* May 2006, and subsequently in *Maybe Baby: 28 Writers Tell the Truth About Skepticism, Infertility, Baby Lust, Childlessness, Ambivalence, and How They Made the Biggest Decision of Their Lives,* edited by Lori Leibovich (New York: Harper-Collins, 2006)

"The Unseen Wind": *More,* April 2008, and subsequently in *About Face: Women Write About What They See When They Look in the Mirror,* edited by Anne Burt and Christina Baker Kline (Berkeley, CA: Seal Press, 2008)

"The Book of My Body": *Allure,* May 2006

"By Angels' Speech and Tongue": *Not Less Than Everything: Catholic Writers on Heroes of Conscience, from Joan of Arc to Oscar Romero,* edited by Catherine Wolff (New York: HarperOne, 2013)

"Mini-Me": *More,* October 2011

"Pilgrim's Progress": *Zoetrope: All-Story,* Fall 2015

About the Author

KATHRYN HARRISON has written the novels *Thicker Than Water, Exposure, Poison, The Binding Chair, The Seal Wife, Envy,* and *Enchantments.* Her autobiographical work includes *The Kiss, Seeking Rapture, The Road to Santiago, The Mother Knot,* and *True Crimes.* She has written two biographies, *Saint Thérèse of Lisieux* and *Joan of Arc,* and a book of true crime, *While They Slept: An Inquiry into the Murder of a Family.* She lives in Brooklyn with her husband, the novelist Colin Harrison.

kathrynharrison.com

Facebook.com/KathrynHarrisonAuthor

About the Type

This book was set in Bembo, a typeface based on an old-style Roman face that was used for Cardinal) Pietro Bembo's tract De Aetna in 1495. Bembo was cut by Francesco Griffo (1450–1518) in the early sixteenth century for Italian Renaissance printer and publisher Aldus Manutius (1449–1515). The Lanston Monotype Company of Philadelphia brought the well-proportioned letterforms of Bembo to the United States in the 1930s.